D0840049

The *Dying Art* of LEADERSHIP

How Leaders Can Help Grieving Employees Excel At Work

GUY CASABLANCA

ANTHONY CASABLANCA

GriefLeaders LLC

Bookbaby Publishing

First Published 2020

Copyright © 2020 Guy and Anthony Casablanca

Print ISBN: 978-1-09832-117-8

Ebook ISBN: 978-1-09832-118-5

Printed in the United States of America

ABOUT THE AUTHORS

Guy Casablanca is a dually licensed funeral director and mortician. He earned his bachelor's degree in mortuary science from the Cincinnati College of Mortuary Science in 1992, where he was recognized for his technical skills and leadership. While formally trained in mortuary science and grief counseling, what makes Guy unique is that he has owned two businesses, consulted for larger corporations, and led teams, divisions, and territories of managers and associates for both privately held and publicly traded companies. Over his career, he has dealt with countless families and extended family members in all facets of the grief process. Guy currently manages a funeral home in Loveland, Colorado, for one of the nation's largest funeral providers.

Anthony Casablanca is an accomplished senior executive, having spent thirty-one years in various leadership roles. Anthony earned his undergraduate degree from Wright State University in Dayton, Ohio, and a master's degree from Kettering University (formerly GMI). Anthony spent most of his years in leadership working for Batesville Casket Company, a recognized leader in the funeral service industry, where he was the vice president of human resources and then the vice president of manufacturing and logistics. Anthony was the 2009 Human Resource Executive of the Year in the state of Indiana. He went on to become president of another subsidiary of the Hillenbrand family of companies. Anthony has spent his entire career studying the art of leadership with an emphasis on purpose-driven leadership principles. Anthony has spoken on several occasions at various funeral industry conventions, was a featured speaker at an international sales, service, and operations meeting for Batesville Casket Company, and has conducted several leadership training classes for funeral providers. After retiring from Hillenbrand Inc., Anthony started Casablanca Consulting LLC to help other organizations and leaders discover their true purpose.

Dedications

To our parents, John and Theresa Casablanca. May this work make you proud of Guy and me — proud of how our relationship has transformed since your passing, and proud of our stewardship of the family name.

To our children, Christopher, Victoria, Alia, and Dominic. May this book serve as a reminder and an example of the importance of family. May it also serve as a piece of our legacy, a glimpse into our hearts and minds, and an example of our desire to help others and make a difference while we were here in some small way.

To Anthony's wife, Linda. You are my soulmate and love of my life. I would not be the person I have become without your love and confidence. I cherish being able to see the world through your eyes.

To Guy's wife, Karen. I don't think anyone can really grasp the level of adversity we have overcome and the odds we beat in our time together. We have suffered both professional and personal losses and have weathered storms of magnitudes that destroy most marriages. I hope this project serves as testimony to what is possible when you have the support of the one you love. Thank you for being my biggest fan and for your unwavering support.

To each other. May this book and our related work serve as a reminder of the promise we made to each other in June of 2010 when the stark reality that what we once called "our family" was now just you and me.

Author's Reading Suggestions

We intentionally wrote this book as a reference guide to leading grieving or emotionally traumatized employees. While all the chapters flow, there is no underlying plot or story that requires you to read the book sequentially. The first half of the book serves as a reference guide for leaders as to the stages of grief, and the emotional state employees will find themselves in when returning to work after a loss or an emotionally traumatizing event. The second half of the book contains an in-depth discussion of the Adaptive Leadership model, how that model integrates into a leader's everyday leadership, as well as how to use the model to help emotionally traumatized employees excel at work. In keeping with the reference guide approach, and to make the reading experience easier, we have included the name of the author under the title of each chapter to help maintain clarity of perspective throughout the book.

Below are three approaches you can take in the reading of this book. Each method has its values and trade-offs to be considered.

The most comprehensive reading experience would be to read the book sequentially and in its entirety. Once completed, return to the beginning and re-read the summaries at the end of each chapter. By reading every chapter sequentially, you will gain the most from the stories, experiences, and examples used to highlight the key learning points.

To capture seventy-five percent of the value of the book, we recommend reading the following chapters entirely and read only the end of chapter summaries of the remaining chapters. We have annotated these chapters with a "star" both in the table of contents and in the chapter headings.

- The Introduction
- Chapter 2 on the Types of Loss

- Chapter 3 on the Stages of Grief
- Chapter 7 on Adaptive Leadership
- Chapter 8 on the Art of Leading Grieving Employees
- Chapter 9 regarding the Person in The Mirror

The final approach to reading this book would be to simply read the introduction and then read all of the end of chapter learning summaries. While this is the most efficient approach, we believe this approach will only yield twenty-five percent of the value of the book.

The fact that you are reading this book at all sets you apart as a leader. We hope you find this to be an insightful read.

TABLE OF CONTENTS

INTRODUCTION *

Why this book is essential and the leadership gap it addresses
(Co-authored)

Here are some sobering facts.

- Every year 2.8 million people die in the United States.[1]
- Every year 2.4 million people go through a divorce in the United States.[2]
- Every year 1.7 million people are diagnosed with cancer in the United States.[3]
- Every year 10.3 million people and their families will deal with the effects of opioid addictions.[4]

The list goes on and on. From the outbreak of mass gun violence to the death of a beloved pet, what do these roughly 17-plus million people and their families have in common? They are all in the grips of grieving and having to deal with an enormous amount of stress, anger, and depression arising from having their lives thrown into extreme turmoil. That means that at a minimum, 47,000 people will show up for work today stressed, angry, depressed, and distracted. Many people in the midst of grieving will say they are looking forward to returning to work in the hopes of regaining some sense of "normalcy" in their life, welcoming the distraction in the hope of preventing them from wallowing in their grief. This very statement is a form of denial. What they really mean is, "*I hope* returning to work will allow me to not deal with my grief during the day." Inevitably, however, their grief creeps to the surface during work, leaving them distracted and confused about the tasks at hand. A once-competent and motivated employee now struggles to handle the responsibilities and pressures of their role.

In reality, that number of 47,000 assumes that only one family member is associated with each of the above statistics, so it is an enormously understated number; it is likely anywhere from two to five times higher. That means the number of people arriving at work today who are experiencing some grief-stricken state could be as high as 235,000 people. The question is, how many of those people will show up to work in your organization today, tomorrow, next month, or this year? For the sake of simplicity, let's assume that these tragedies do impact only one person. That would mean that 5.2 percent of the US population of some 331 million people is experiencing some form of grief. Stated another way, for every 100 employees in your organization, five people are struggling with the effects of grief.

A study conducted by The Grief Recovery Institute and reported on by the *Chicago Tribune* estimates that the loss of productivity due to employees grieving a loss could be as high as $75 billion a year.[5] The study also revealed the following insights:

- Illness or deaths in the family are the second most common problems affecting workforce performance.
- 90 percent of people in physical jobs report a much higher incidence of physical injuries due to reduced concentration in the weeks or months following a loss.
- 70 percent of grieving people surveyed report increased or new use of alcohol or mood-altering substances up to six months or more following a significant loss.
- 90 percent of grieving people surveyed report a reduction in their ability to concentrate following a loss.
- Grief isn't limited to the death of a loved one. Workers may be affected by many different types of loss, such as a pet's death, a divorce, house fire or theft, or family crises.
- While grief is the normal and natural reaction to loss, it is typically not resolved by the time workers return from a bereavement leave. The

initial shock of a loved one's death is usually just wearing off, and true grieving has just begun. That means workers will be grieving while they are doing their jobs.

More importantly, this leads to a second and third question. Are the leaders in your organization, or any organization, prepared to _**LEAD**_ these people when they return to work? And, does your organization have a formalized framework to train its leaders on this topic or a process for leaders to follow when having to lead grieving employees? In our experience, the answer is usually a resounding _"NO."_ Leadership training typically does not address this issue. As a result, at best, leaders "deal with" the situation, and at worst, leaders ignore the grief process as if the employee can switch it off and leave their grief at home.

This book attempts to help leaders and organizations understand what happens when a significant loss occurs and help leaders develop the skills to LEAD an employee as they struggle through the grief process. When applied, we believe what you will learn in this book will engender a higher level of commitment, engagement, and loyalty in the grieving employee. It will also help to ensure that your organization does not bear its share of the $75 billion productivity loss associated with the devastation your employees feel when they experience a loss.

Additionally, the concepts presented in this book extend well beyond the scenarios of grief and emotionally traumatic events. These concepts apply broadly and should be integrated into the way you lead. If you do this, you will see your team's results, morale, engagement, and commitment improve.

We would like to share one caveat. While it is not our intent to focus this book solely on the grief associated with death, the grieving process is most easily identifiable with this type of loss. As such, many of the examples cited do speak about death-related loss. This is done to drive home the critical principles of leading a grieving employee and is not intended to minimize the effects of all the other types of loss that cause employees to grieve.

"Business doesn't prepare us for the presence of death at the office. The business schools don't teach anything about it, about what the manager says when someone says, 'I have cancer,' or about what to say to the other employees who will have to spend days and days with this constant reminder of their own mortality."

—James Autry, business leader and author, from his book *Confessions of an Accidental Businessman*

CHAPTER 1

Moribund

A Prelude by Guy Casablanca
The overlap between funeral directing and leadership

"I'm a funeral director," I said.

"Like … you … work on the dead?" he responded with a trepidatious pause.

"No. Like, I work on the *living* when someone they love has died."

My profession raises eyebrows and sparks curiosity in nearly everyone who asks me, "So what do you do?" And to a certain extent, I accommodate their natural, morbid desire to know just what goes on behind the curtain of a mortuary establishment. But it's a hard conversation to sustain because, in all reality, the gory details of the postmortem care I provide are minuscule in comparison to the amount of time and energy that I invest in the living, rather than the dead.

I cannot think of any occupation or profession more misunderstood than funeral directing. People picture a grim and depressing environment in a funeral home: one of dimly lit rooms and the overpowering scent of flowers, decrepit crypt keepers, and softly played, solemn organ music. They imagine the shadow of death lurking in every corner and conversations quietly whispered in hushed tones, as not to arouse the spirit of the Grim Reaper himself.

The clients I deal with are often pleasantly surprised when they leave a conference with me. Surprised by the upscale cleanliness and lighting reminiscent of a fine hotel. Surprised by the amicable and friendly nature of the staff.

1

Surprised by the open, honest, and diverse course of the conversation. Surprised by the fact that their preconceived notions fell away so quickly. Often clients expect our meeting to be painful, sad, and regrettable. They do not expect to leave feeling relieved and confident about the difficult process that lies ahead. They don't expect to gain an insight into their loved one, themselves, or even the nature of life itself. They don't expect to feel "good" about things.

Through diligent work and years of refinement, I have learned how to serve and guide suffering people to bring them to a mental state that will allow for healthy grieving to happen naturally. By crafting a very deliberate approach to the complicated subject and complex situation of loss, I have honed a precise method of communicating with the grieving. I have developed a carefully orchestrated process that allows me to conduct business while catering to the specific needs of a devastated and broken soul.

I intend to share with you the aspects of my job that overlap with yours. It may not seem obvious that we have much in common, but in fact, we do.

Arranging a funeral requires massive amounts of the truest form of leadership. That is to say, success as a funeral director comes from building people up, inspiring them, and gently directing them toward a goal that benefits themselves more than me. For me to enjoy one small benefit, like a modest raise or a performance bonus, I must create massive benefits for hundreds of other people. In doing so, I create a positive feedback loop. If business with me creates a benefit in *your* life, you'll come back to do business with me again. And the more that loop repeats, the more benefits I reap as well.

This book is meant to inspire you to exercise your truest leadership—to dig deep into your best abilities to anticipate, communicate, and accommodate; to plan for the difficult while it is still easy to engage inevitable challenges before they become unanticipated obstacles; and to lead through difficult circumstances when everyone else walks away.

This daily part of my job is our common ground. There will come a day, I assure you, when you will need to lead people through dark times. You may define "dark times" however you like. It may be as obvious as the death of a valued employee or their spouse or child, or as covert as the depressed state of the nation during a deep recession or crumbling mortgage economy. You and your company, no matter how big or small, will assuredly face "dark times" that require exceptional and adaptive leadership skills.

So read the following pages knowing you are acquiring a toolset that is adaptable to *many* different situations, not just death within or close to your organization. The principles, strategies, and processes outlined here will prove an invaluable resource regarding a topic that few people are willing to address, so kudos to you for being in the top percentile of leaders willing to tackle this topic before it is needed. You are among a rare few who acknowledge that the best leaders are defined not by their ability to guide people through ordinary times but by their ability to guide people through the *worst* of times successfully—without losing productivity or profitability, and by making people who are down and out feel empowered and uplifted.

"If there ever comes a day where we can't be together, keep me in your heart. I'll stay there forever."

—A. A. Milne, author
of *Winnie the Pooh*

CHAPTER 2
The Types of Loss *

Helping leaders understand that not all losses are created equal
(Guy Casablanca)

Like the unpredictability of the ocean, the relatively calm waters on the surface of our lives do not reveal the turbulent undercurrents and riptides that lie beneath. At first glance, loss and grief seem quite simple to recognize and define. But more profound than the superficial definitions we have come to know and recognize, an emotional torrent of rapidly moving currents is shifting and changing, with the potential to become a breaking wave of whitewater and destruction.

Loss is a complex creature. It wears many faces and comes in many forms. The loss of a loved one or treasured friend is an obvious predecessor to grief and bereavement. But loss takes many shapes and is delivered in packages of all sizes. What may seem insignificant to one person may have profound emotional ramifications on another. Therefore, it is crucial to understand the very nature of grief itself.

First and foremost, we must realize that when we *celebrate* something in life, we celebrate a moment, like a wedding or an anniversary, a graduation or a birthday. It is a fleeting moment, usually just one day long, that represents a culmination of events or an accomplishment in our lives. Although the celebration may be years in the making, take months of planning, and include weeks of swelling anticipation, the celebration itself comes and goes in a matter of hours.

In stark contrast, when we *grieve* over something, we digress into the sadness of *everything we have ever lost in our lifetime*. When my father died, I relived the loss of my grandparents all over again. When my mother died, I relived the grief of my father's death. When the house I grew up in was sold, I relived the loss of my mother again. The same happened when my dog died, when my aunt died, and when my college friend died. Each loss opened the scars of losses from my past, beckoned long-repressed sadness to the surface, and forced me to reflect on an entire lifetime of losses. The event that triggered these feelings was but a moment in time. The feelings themselves were buried for years.

Why is this? Twenty years had elapsed between my father's death and my mother's passing. This certainly seems like ample time to have come to terms with one loss before incurring another of equal magnitude. And why did the death of my aunt make me cry over my mom again? I rarely ever saw my aunt; I hadn't seen her at all in at least eight years. How broken up could I possibly be over a long-distance relative passing? Why did it dig up old emotions and bring past sadness to the surface?

The reason we grieve so deeply is that we never get *over* our losses; we just get *through* them. The resiliency of the basic human instinct to survive makes us push forward, even if it means repressing our feelings so we can take care of our obligations, be there for our kids' sporting events, pay our bills, and get back to work. More often than not, what we consider "dealing well" with adversity and loss is just a masquerade we perform to get on with our daily lives. Under the surface, a swelling current of emotions is whirling around, manifesting itself in our dreams, in our subconscious thoughts, in our subtle actions, and in the way we react when a new loss comes along.

Within a professional organization, virtually every type of loss will need to be addressed at some point. Not every loss is dealt with in the same way, and it is important to quantify the depth and breadth of the situation in order to lead people through it effectively. We will discuss principles of leadership through the grieving process in later chapters. For now, let's just focus on the situational aspects of the types of loss an organization will inevitably encounter.

Natural, Anticipated, and Expected Losses

Some things are lingering on the horizon of our lives that can be seen from miles away. My mom was first diagnosed with breast cancer in 1991. She, and our family, knew that even though this was a treatable and survivable condition, it meant she would one day have to battle cancer again … and she did. Around 2006, cancer reared its ugly head again, and a new, more difficult battle for her life began. She fought it well. Five years later, she was still treating and battling the grips of metastatic cancer, but we all knew that one day the fight would come to an end. My mother was brazenly honest about her condition, saying that she would eventually decide that the sickness of chemotherapy would not be worth the quality of life she had left, and she would make the choice to stop fighting and accept her fate openly. She faced this reality on June 11, 2010, when she gave in to the deadliness of this relentless disease.

Her death crushed me.

Although it had been coming for years, and regardless of the myriad of signs that death was on the horizon, when the days leading to her death arrived, I wasn't ready to let go. We had said everything we could ever want to say to each other. We'd had considerable time to prepare, and we took advantage of that time. Our last spoken words to each other, before she was kept sedate in a state of drug-induced "comfort," were "I love you." As far as she and our family were concerned, she had beaten cancer because she enjoyed the hell out of her limited time, fought till the end, and went out on her own terms and at a time she felt was appropriate. It was one of the most well-orchestrated end-of-life scenarios I had ever seen and the most graceful ending anyone could ever hope for.

Nonetheless, I was devastated. Her passing was a harsh reminder that I was now parentless. Even though I was forty years old, well established in my career, and had long since been "on my own" in life, the emotional security of her wisdom and support was forever gone. When my wife would call her mom to chat, I would cry. When something good happened in my life that I wanted to share, I would cry. When something troubled me, and I needed to vent, I would cry. When my daughter would say, "I miss Grandma Terry," I would cry.

Anticipated losses of natural causes, as expected as they are, can also be no less significant than tragic, unexpected circumstances.

There is a quote I love: "All farewells should be sudden." I mention it because expected; anticipated death is not necessarily to anyone's advantage. Sometimes the anticipation of the inevitable only causes us to delay experiencing our pent-up emotions. I know I started grieving when I first learned my mom had cancer. For a long time, I repressed the sadness it brought me in an effort to "stay strong" for her. But when "farewell" finally reached my doorstep, I was not ready to say goodbye, and my years of grief over the battle she faced, husbandless, widowed, and alone, came rushing to the top of my mental state when she took her last breath. The success of her battle against cancer was merely a Band-Aid on the reality of the situation, and part of me wishes it had been torn off quickly rather than over several years.

When my mom's mother died, years later, at the ripe old age of ninety-nine, I shed a tear accompanied by a sentimental smile in honor of the fact that her incredible life journey had ended. But I was now faced with yet another new reality: there were no more generations above me on my family tree. My brother and I would be the next to go.

What happened? It seems like yesterday I was just a wee little branch at the bottom of that tree, and now here I am, the next leaf to fall from the very top. My grandmother's death was not only expected, inevitable, anticipated, and natural, but it was outright *unbelievable* that she had outlived almost everyone in the family! And although she woke up every day wondering just why in the hell she was still alive, when she died, I was deeply moved for reasons that were beyond the isolated event of her passing. It changed my perception of my place in life and escorted my own mortality ever closer to my everyday reality.

Do not underestimate the emotional impact of an anticipated, expected, and natural loss. There are other factors to consider that may not be obvious on the surface.

Unnatural, Unanticipated, and Unexpected Losses

When a child, sibling, or a member of the younger generation dies suddenly and unexpectedly, the loss becomes far more complex. Grief of this magnitude can instigate a period of shock that lasts for years, and what some may interpret as "healthy grieving" might actually signify repressed feelings in disguise.

Our psyche does not know how to process a loss that feels unnatural. A parent should never have to bury a child. It breaks the natural order of what we know to be true in this world. We expect older people to die first, not the other way around.

I know this scenario all too well, as my career as a funeral director has ushered into my office those affected by such tragic circumstances many, many times. I often encounter parents who look like they have not quite woken up from a deep sleep, with glazed eyes and expressionless faces, short on words and unable to think clearly, perpetually trapped in a state of confusion and forgetfulness. They struggle to remember the simplest things, like the names of their other children, their own address, or phone numbers. Answers are delayed behind long pauses. Stuttering, stammering, and searching for words, replies are often inaccurate and incomplete.

And yet other parents are entirely engaged in preparing for the funeral, with extensive notes that detail every minute aspect of the services they would like. They are seemingly organized and focused and, from all outward appearances, look like they are dealing quite well with what has happened.

But under the surface, an inverse relationship is unfolding. The disconnected, foggy-minded parents are enveloped in their grief and emotions and simply cannot deal with the reality of the tasks at hand as they move through the grieving process. To the contrary, the hyper-focused parents are suppressing their innermost emotions and grief by enveloping themselves in a task-oriented mind frame. Eventually, a flip will occur, when the foggy-minded people snap out of it, and the focused parents will snap backward into grief.

My experience has taught me that the prior scenario is the most likely and the most natural. The latter is a warning sign of a state of denial that needs to be taken seriously. The longer someone lingers in a state of denial, the greater will be the recoil that follows. In other words, the bigger they are, the harder they fall. Someone who's personality demands that they shut things out and focus, focus, focus will eventually hit a wall where they cannot deny their feelings any longer, and a big emotional wave will come crashing down on them. That will likely occur after their bereavement leave from work is over and they are mid-project at work, months after the loss has occurred.

In contrast, the person who has been wrought with grief for weeks and weeks, obviously unable to process effectively, will eventually regain the composure to "pull it together" and move forward.

We'll discuss the fluidity and ramifications of the standard grief model in the next chapter, but for now, just know that the sheer trauma of an unexpected, unanticipated loss will often mask the true state of a person's grief.

Tragic Circumstances

An unexpected loss can be further complicated by the modality of the person's death. Homicide, suicide, and accidental deaths bring a level of sensitivity with them that is especially difficult to navigate. These types of losses span all ages, and I have seen many a situation where an elderly person died unnecessarily at the hands of tragedy. This is ground where the anticipated loss and the unexpected nature of death collide violently. Sure, we knew grandma would *eventually* die, but to be killed in a tragic accident brings about a level of grief that would not normally accompany the loss of a person her age.

I encountered such a situation when the mother of a coworker wandered off from her home. She was in her mid-seventies and getting senile. The family was deliberating diligently over whether to have her admitted to an assisted living facility where she could be checked on more frequently. A care facility was outside their financial means, so it was a difficult decision. Before they could come to terms with how to pay for the aging woman's care, she disappeared. Local news outlets reported her missing, unsure if she had been abducted or was just lost. Days turned into weeks, and weeks turned into months. Eventually, my coworker's mother was found in a field, badly decomposed and fully clothed, except for the loss of one shoe. Apparently, she had wandered into the middle of nowhere, collapsed from hunger and exhaustion, and died. She laid there for approximately nine weeks before being discovered.

This situation falls within the complicated realm of an anticipated, yet tragic and unexpected loss. The aging woman was showing signs of decline, and the eventuality of her death was coming to light, but the modality of her demise was wrought with complicated emotional triggers, being both untimely and tragic.

The way the company reacted to this circumstance is a major contributing factor to why I felt compelled to collaborate with my brother on writing this book. The daughter of this poor woman was devastated, wrestling with both guilt and grief simultaneously. We worked in a very demanding, corporately controlled call center together. The very nature of that job requires lightning-fast reaction time, complete clarity, unfettered focus, and a polite and cheerful disposition, even when dealing with the worst callers.

I could tell that my coworker was not ready to return to the floor immediately after her mother's closed-casket funeral. She needed time and space to process things, to grieve, and to start the healing process. But she had to return to work or risk losing her job. With a tear in her eye, she explained her situation to me as she made her way to her cubicle on her third day back. She thanked me for being the only person willing to talk to her about how she felt and her situation. Nobody at work wanted anything to do with this conversation. Coworkers avoided her. Management hardly addressed the circumstances. Even her friends dodged the topic.

I found this type of reaction to be unnatural and unnecessary. Everyone who worked there, and the company as a whole, treated the situation as though ignoring it would make it go away for the grieving associate. This only added to her isolated feelings and inability to deal with her emotions.

On the level of the associates, I wouldn't expect much different. They are largely untrained and unprepared to converse with and offer comfort to someone in a deep state of grief. The company, on the other hand, should have been more prepared. After all, this was an international organization with thousands of employees. How was it that they had never come up with a plan for addressing these situations? They didn't have any leeway on their bereavement policy to accommodate the unique nature of this situation, and they made a veteran associate return to work in a mental state that made her an outright liability to the organization.

It is said that an employee will never treat a client any better than the company is treating that employee. Just as an invaluable employee is identified by their ability to perform at peak levels in times of great adversity, an invaluable company with invaluable leadership will be determined by their ability to address the most difficult and uncomfortable circumstances.

I interpreted this particular company's mismanagement of the situation as a sign of poor leadership and poor policy. Within days of the above described events, I resigned and, in no unclear terms, communicated exactly why I was leaving. My reasoning and intuition proved correct. It took some years to play itself out, but today, that company, which had nearly global market influence and offices all over North America and Europe, no longer exists. It fell victim not to competition but to internal decay and mismanagement that didn't allow the company to remain competitive. The writing was on the wall with the way the company handled the tragic grief of one employee in one lone call center.

Combined Losses

As you can imagine, each of these types of loss can overlap into multiple categories, and with each confluence of circumstances comes a different set of parameters that apply toward moving through the grief process.

Natural but unanticipated losses are among the most complex, hovering in the ranks of unexpected and tragic deaths. I see this all the time as a mortician.

Here is a natural, but unanticipated example: To my trained eye, there may be no mystery surrounding a death. The person was overweight, showed signs of diminished circulation in their lower extremities, and had scars from surgeries they should not have needed at their age. But a fatal heart attack at forty-five years of age is nevertheless going to send a family into a state of shock and disbelief, even though the warning signs were obvious.

Here is an anticipated, but unexpected example: A ten-year-old girl has a congenital heart defect. The condition is generally not life-threatening, but her parents know that this abnormality will shorten her overall lifespan as she matures. They monitor her activity closely and do all they can to protect her from this condition. But despite their best efforts, she collapses on the school playground and dies in front of all her classmates.

Here is an anticipated, but tragic example: A family member has wrestled with substance abuse for decades. The family has long since disowned and disavowed the habitual abuser since his teen years, and by his mid-twenties, he was banished from the family altogether and practically homeless. Every one of his relatives is surprised that his body has not given in to the abuse or fallen victim to neglect. But when that person commits suicide, the trauma of the death is rarely diminished by the circumstances that precluded the event for years on end.

I could continue with examples that will take your breath away. I've worked on many a seventy-year-old, terminally ill suicide case. I've seen dozens of young people fall victim to their own bad habits and weaknesses. The point is, overlapping circumstances will quickly become complicated grieving processes.

The grieving person's personality type, position in the company, job demands, and personal life will all add to the complexity of the leadership skills you will need to apply. It is imperative to have a thorough understanding of the stages of grief and the nature of the grieving process to assess the situation appropriately and adapt your leadership model accordingly.

No two situations will be exactly the same. No two people will react and grieve in exactly the same way. You will need to be as fluid as the grieving process itself, and your emotional awareness needs to be at its keenest. After all, your associates, your departments and divisions, and virtually the entire organization are watching to see how the company handles this situation. How did the company react? What steps did they take? What gestures did they make? How did they recognize not only the loss but the people affected by it?

The answers to these questions will vary depending on the type of loss, the person lost, and the people left grieving. But the very first step is understanding the grief process itself.

Types of Loss Chapter Summary

- We never get over our losses…we just get through them.
- Do not underestimate the emotional impact of an anticipated, expected, and natural loss. There are other factors to consider that may not be obvious on the surface.

- A company with invaluable leadership will be determined by its ability to address the most challenging and uncomfortable circumstances, not by their ability to respond to the status quo.

- No two situations will be exactly the same. No two people will react and grieve exactly the same. You will need to be as fluid as the grieving process itself, and your emotional awareness needs to be at its keenest.

- It is imperative to have a thorough understanding of the stages of grief and the nature of the grieving process itself to assess the situation appropriately and adapt your leadership model accordingly.

"It's so curious: one can resist tears and 'behave' very well in the hardest hours of grief. But then someone makes you a friendly sign behind a window, or one notices that a flower that was in bud only yesterday has suddenly blossomed, or a letter slips from a drawer … and everything collapses."

—Colette, author of *The Tendrils of the Vine*

CHAPTER 3
The Stages of Grief*

Helping leaders recognize the connection between an employee's emotional state, their performance, the stages of grief and how leadership matters at this moment
(Guy Casablanca)

Before beginning this chapter, I feel both compelled and obligated to mention a pertinent fact. I am *not* a licensed therapist or a certified grief counselor. My personal, firsthand experience in dealing with loss, grief, and grieving people is different from that of a licensed therapist or counselor, and in some ways far more extensive.

According to a response to this question on the question-and-answer website Quora.com, a reputable and busy licensed therapist or grief counselor may work with fifty or sixty individual clients repeatedly over the course of a year. As a licensed funeral director, I will counsel fifty or sixty individual grieving people in a matter of a few weeks, and five hundred or so individual people in a year.

I have suffered personal losses of both tragic and natural circumstances myself. I have helped guide people through the grief process as it applies to every conceivable manner of death and loss imaginable. I have helped facilitate healthy grieving for countless numbers of people, and I have witnessed utterly unhealthy grieving in a rare few. I have dealt with grieving children, teens, and adults alike, in unfathomable quantities. And unlike grief counselors, psychologists, and therapists, I encounter people's grief in the moment the loss has occurred. Most therapists and counselors will begin seeing clients weeks or months after the loss has occurred. I, to the contrary, see them in the moment. Often, the first time they are seeing their deceased loved one is when I personally walk them into the visitation room at the funeral home. I counsel them within hours of being notified of someone's death, not weeks or months later. I deal with grieving people in their most emotional state, and I have to break news to them that they may not want to hear, such as "I'm sorry, but due to the extensive nature of your mom's accident, I would not recommend seeing her in her current condition." I also need to do all this while I write up a contract for funeral services and gracefully ask them for a check to pay for it all.

So I repeat: I am not a licensed therapist or grief counselor. I have a different and arguably broader set of experiences than that. With that established, let us look at the stages of grief from the perspective of someone who knows them intimately, firsthand, day in, day out.

Most people are familiar with the psychiatrist Elisabeth Kübler-Ross's five-stage model of grief.[1] It is commonly accepted as the "standard" model and typically includes denial, anger, bargaining, depression, and acceptance. For our purposes, we will forgo the history of the model and the elaborate explanations of every stage, as their definitions are self-evident in the terms used to identify them. For the sake of brevity:

- *Denial* identifies the immediate stage of shock and disbelief that the loss has occurred.
- *Anger* typically follows denial as a natural reaction to being let down.
- *Bargaining* is commonly accompanied by statements of regret and questioning the circumstances surrounding the situation: "If only I had (done something)." "We should have (whatever)."
- *Depression* is usually the indication that the reality of the situation is setting in.
- *Acceptance* comes when all else falls away and the grieving person is capable of moving forward in their new reality.

There is another stage of grief that is rarely addressed and perhaps one of the most critical:

– *Sharing* what you have learned with others.

Before we delve into the individual stages and their implications, it is important to note that the grieving process can actually begin *before* the loss has occurred. In such a case, you will need to exercise your strategic, adaptive leadership skills with a certain amount of forethought involved.

For example, say an assistant manager of a small, start-up retail operation is nursing his stepmother through the end-of-life phases as her battle with cancer comes to a close. He is perpetually tired, often late to work, and sometimes doesn't show up at all, without notice, as his body is too exhausted to even hear his alarm in the morning. People dying of cancer or enduring dementia often go through a syndrome called sundowners syndrome, where panic and anxiety set in just before nighttime arrives and an irritable state of insomnia takes over until the sun returns. It's a real phenomenon, and this phase of the dying process has the assistant manager up all night, trying to comfort and console his terminal family member.

The assistant manager is grieving already, but it's not apparent at first. From all outward appearances, he is just not performing well. He is acting irresponsibly compared to the dedication of the other employees, and they are getting tired of covering for his shortcomings.

And you, as the general manager or owner of the operation, have a business to run. Many owners do not take a salary until the business is profitable, so the assistant manager is literally the only person profiting from this hypothetical start-up business, and he is not earning his keep or living up to his obligations.

Other employees are talking. One of the best of them quits and goes to work for a competitor, stating in no uncertain terms that the reason he is leaving is because he feels like he has to perform to a standard of quality that his immediate superior does not have to meet. In his eyes, the assistant manager can do whatever the hell he wants without repercussion. And to a certain extent, he is right.

A coup is brewing in your organization. It's becoming evident that the entire workforce is now intolerant of the lack of reliability they are experiencing in their direct supervisor, the assistant manager.

To save the business and salvage what remaining good employees you have, you tell the assistant manager that despite his valid reasons, he is not living up to the expectations of his job, and he is relieved of his duties. Effectively, he is fired, immediately.

He understands. He is regretful that he let the operation down. He believes he should have done more to communicate with the owner and find a way to arrange coverage for his absences.

There is one more important factor to note about this scenario. It's not hypothetical. That business was mine, and I was the owner and manager.

I started the business with the inheritance that came to me when my mother died. I had taken no salary for the first year and had sunk everything I had into getting this start-up off the ground. I hired a very close friend to be my assistant manager. And when he was under immense stress, caring for his dying stepmother, I let him down. I fired him.

At the time, it felt like the right thing to do to save my business and send a message to my other employees that, in this day and age of technology, there was no reason to miss a workday without calling in. The assistant manager, because he was so mentally exhausted, was making mistakes that created huge liabilities for my business. His dying stepmother was not my problem. My problem was that if I didn't get this ship on the right course, I would lose my employees, my business, and my money in one fell swoop. I had to take swift and stern action to let everyone in the company know that I would not be swayed by emotions, no matter how pure, no matter how valid, no matter how desperate. I wanted them to know that I meant business and was not to be taken lightly.

You're probably squirming in your seat at the heartlessness of this story. Unfortunately, I did not have the guidance I am offering you under my belt at the time. *Oh, how I could have used this book in that moment!*

The right thing to do would have been to rally my employees and explain the situation to them, ask for their help in supporting our assistant manager, ask for their patience, and maybe even incentivize them with bonuses for the person who did the most to keep us on track while our coworker did what he needed to do. I failed as a leader.

When I decided to co-author this book, I called that friend of mine, my past assistant manager. I invited him to my home, and over a cold beer on my patio, I apologized. I told him I'd handled that situation all wrong, and I regretted it. I was blinded by my business, consumed with the concept of getting out of the red and into the black, and I prioritized myself over him—probably the least leadership-focused thing I could have done.

Thankfully, he accepted my apology. When I said I was wrong, he simply said, "I know. You were wrong. But you had a business to run. And honestly, Guy, I respected you for having the guts to do what you did. It taught me a lesson about not taking my position or my friends for granted. I let you down, and I'm sorry too."

We hugged, clinked our beer bottles together, and moved forward. He is one of my closest friends to this day, and I have since created other opportunities for him, in which he has performed exceptionally well. He continues to enjoy great success in his current occupation, partially because of the hard lesson he learned from my mistakes as a leader.

If nothing else, he learned that working under poor leadership is a recipe for doom, inevitably destined to fall apart.

In that scenario, I failed to realize that my friend was already grieving. I failed to inquire deeply enough about his life to understand how to help him. I was only focused on what *he* could do for *me*.

Now, back to the grief model. It has five stages that can begin before the loss has even occurred.

The first two stages of grief can be thought of as the "stunting stages." As I have experienced myself, denial and anger will lock a person in a mental state that stunts their personal and emotional growth, preventing any real progress in nearly all of life's many facets. Relationships will suffer. Pursuits will be hindered. Goals will be diverted. Momentum will be lost. My assistant manager was in this stunting stage of grief. I should have recognized this from personal experience.

For myself, the unexpected loss of my father during my formative teen years left me extremely angry. I didn't *feel* angry, but in retrospect, all my self-destructive habits started immediately after his death. I had never smoked before that, but I started smoking, in utter spite of the fact that all of the men in my family died of cardiovascular or smoking-related diseases. I had never drunk alcohol, but I started drinking as a way to feel like I was living life to the fullest. I had never done drugs, but I started experimenting with *everything* as a way to expand my mind beyond what I knew as my current reality. I had never gotten into trouble, but I started delving into the dark underworld of criminal elements as a way of rebelling against a society that I viewed as unfair. And as for relationships … forget it. I was cruising through women at a record pace, unable to find happiness with anyone I dated. This was because I was unhappy, but I didn't know it. My relationship with my mother was extremely strained. I couldn't seem to get along with any of my bosses, and I changed career paths every few months.

In hindsight, I was stuck in a combative stage of anger for literally a decade. It completely stunted my personal, professional, and romantic growth. I found myself, at twenty-nine years old, stuck in the mentality of a teenager who still thought he was invincible, untouchable, inarguable, and immortal. It was not until I was thirty years old that I realized how angry I had been all those years. I was, literally, stunted by grief.

Further confirmation of the stymieing nature of grief and loss was illustrated to me by a close friend. Let's call him "Bob." Bob was fifty years old but had a boyish quality about him that was reminiscent of a child in elementary school. His expressions and mannerisms were textbook adolescent. His pattern of speech and cadence was prepubescent. His emotional vulnerability and concern for what others thought of him were characteristic of schoolchildren. Mind you, these traits were part of his charm and personality, and I never really gave them a second thought. That is, until we had a very personal conversation about his upbringing.

Bob was raised in a very strict Southern Baptist household by a Bible-thumping mother who preached fire and brimstone at every pass. He recalled being locked in a dark closet to pray for forgiveness over things that were trivial and natural for a child to do. Getting his school clothes dirty, spilling a drink on the carpet, and rolling his eyes were things punishable by not only long hours locked in a prayer closet, but by savage beatings as well. He was only a child, roughly eight or nine years old.

It all made sense now. He was traumatized by the loss of faith he had in his mother. She beat him into a state of submission, and without proper guidance and counseling to deal with such trauma, he was forever stunted by his grief, perpetually trapped in the mind of a child and unable to mature, to progress, and to accomplish.

He is now sixty years old, still single, never having had a genuinely emotional and mature relationship. He is still lost professionally, having never accomplished anything substantial in his career. He is still cautious and concerned and worried about people's perceptions of him. To this very day, he has remained locked in grief, even though he cannot fathom the idea that he may be trapped in the stunting stages of the Kübler-Ross model. What happened in his childhood is water under the bridge as far as he's concerned, and in his mind, he has long since moved on. But in all reality, he hasn't.

When a member of your team suffers a loss, you can expect them, at least momentarily, to be stunted by their grief. Everything will come to a screeching halt until they can move through their disbelief and anger and into the next two stages, bargaining and depression, which I refer to as the discovery stages.

When we start bargaining with reality, we begin to question our actions and how we handled certain things that we feel may have contributed to the loss we are suffering. This is not necessarily a bad thing, because it can bring to light our own shortcomings and character flaws. Perhaps our bargaining questions are a far stretch from reality, but maybe, just *maybe*, they are spot on.

"If only I had been a better friend and listened more than I spoke."

"I should have taken him to the doctor when we first had an issue."

"I wonder if his stress level at home had anything to do with this?"

Being a more understanding and present friend, being too complacent about health issues, and being mindful of how we affect those around us are all valid personality traits to question and improve upon. It may come at a high price, but the bargaining stage of grief can inspire personal growth and trigger changes that are long overdue, making us better people in the end.

Some bargaining questions may be spawned from regret and may not be valid at all. It is up to you as a leader to encourage growth and negate self-doubt by eliminating questions that do not promote healing and a healthy emotional state. We often say things like, "You can't think that way," and that is sometimes a valid response. We are not omnipotent creatures, and yet in hindsight we believe we should have been all-knowing and smarter in the moment.

It is a delicate affair to address legitimate bargaining questions, and doing so is ***ONLY*** within the realm of a professional counselor. It can trigger an angry response, so it is safest to allow the grieving individual to voice their frustrations and questions and let them come to terms with what is the ultimate truth themselves. It is not advisable to agree with them, no matter how true their statement may be. "Yeah, you probably should have" is never a good thing to say when someone is working their way through grief-inflicted self-discovery.

Like bargaining, depression can be a phase of discovery. Have you ever noticed how an artist's most compelling works so often come from times of darkness in their lives? Some of the greatest love songs ever composed are written after breakups. Some of the best works of art arise from times of great pain in the artist's life, or are expressions of extremely dark subject matter. Some of the best stories and movies and poems are a direct reflection of the creator's sadness.

Depression often carries nothing beyond a negative connotation. It has been stigmatized with a perception of loneliness, self-neglect, isolation, and even suicide. But depression is natural. We all get depressed sometimes. How we deal with our depression is what makes or breaks us. It is okay to be depressed, especially after a loss. What drives most people to the extremes of depression is that nobody wants to deal with or be around a depressed person, which amplifies their feelings of loneliness and despair.

It is important to recognize someone's depression and empathize with it. A sympathetic ear can go a long way toward turning depression into a growth opportunity. Suicide hotlines realize this. It is amazing how someone's attitude can change if you just let them talk. More often than not, they will discover for themselves that they alone are responsible for their emotions and feelings, and that all this grief they are feeling is only temporary. A gentle reminder that "the only consistent thing in life is change itself" may help. Grief and depression are temporary.

It is *not* okay to *ignore* depression, personally or in others. But you need to allow depression to run its course. If you recognize that the cycle is spiraling downward, professional intervention may be necessary. Most companies have programs in place to help people in desperate situations. I implore you to make sure your organization has and utilizes such resources and encourages your associates to take advantage of such programs if necessary.

Finally, we come to the growth phases of the grief cycle. These are acceptance and sharing what you've learned with others.

Acceptance is indicative of growth itself. This is evidenced by the usual first stage of recovery from addiction: admitting you have a problem. You must first admit to and accept the problem if you're ever going to move beyond it. Accepting a loss is essentially accepting the problem that has had you in a state of grief.

Acceptance comes with time and with diligent, deliberate work on one's self. Acceptance comes from honest reflection and helpful guidance. Acceptance is the goal—the end result of the soul-crushing stages of grief that precede it. Acceptance is typically hallmarked by a sense of relief, but do not automatically assume the sense of relief that comes at the end of a long and painful battle with an affliction is true acceptance of the loss.

When my father died at the end of a debilitating end of life process, there was a certain sense of relief that accompanied his passing, as the pain, suffering, and dehumanizing nature of his condition were over for him. This was not to say I was even remotely accepting of his untimely death.

True acceptance, as stated, takes time. Grieving individuals tend to mask their pain by jumping right to the acceptance phase for the sake of emotional convenience. ***This is denial, not acceptance***.

This is why it is imperative to recognize the stages of grief, to be able to identify them, and to know where someone is in the grief process. A sudden jump to a more advanced state is indicative of a false positive, if you will.

This can be seen in suicidal individuals. When someone suddenly jumps from a state of deep depression to a sense of happiness, an alarm should go off. If such a sudden jump is also accompanied by unusual gestures, like giving away personal items of sentimental value, then *bells and alarms* should go off! This is common among people on the very brink of suicide. Their despair suddenly evaporates when they have committed fully to the idea of killing themselves. There is no longer a need to be sad because the end of the suffering has a date and time associated with it, and they know this will all be over soon. The person begins to say goodbye in subtle ways like making amends with people they know will be hurt by their decision, and by giving away things they hope will become treasured keepsakes to the recipient. These gestures help the depressed, suicidal person feel good about their decision and provide relief to the person's long battle with depression and self-destructive contemplation. The happiness these gestures bring to others validates their preconceived notion that they have been a burden on those around them and bolsters their decision to follow through with their own suicide.

Beware of sudden jumps in progress. They are rarely true indications of progress but rather masking techniques employed out of desperation.

Now that we have identified the various stages of grief, it should be evident that they apply to nearly any and every loss that we experience in our lives, be it the loss of a loved one or a pet, the loss of a relationship or a sentimental object, or even the loss of a major account or losing a championship game.

When my professional endeavors allow me the time, I coach youth hockey as a way of staying in shape and reconnecting with my passion for the world's most exciting game (some may beg to differ about that last comment). I see the five stages of grief play out in my team when they suffer a major loss on the ice.

Denial: *"I can't believe we lost!"*

Anger: *"Dammit! We freakin' LOST!"*

Bargaining: *"If only we had passed the puck more! I wish we had a different referee! We could have beat them on our home ice!"*

Depression: *"I'm never playing hockey again. I suck at this game."*

Acceptance: *"We'll get 'em next time!"*

And the sixth stage: *"Let me tell you why we lost to those guys."*

Notice how the bargaining stage provided personal insight, and this discovery revealed a weakness that could lead to improvement. *"We should have passed the puck more."*

A loss is a loss is a loss. No matter the situation, the grief model, to some degree, always applies. It is ingrained in our psychological recesses and always manages to rear its head somehow. One of the ways psychologists identify psychosis in young children is when the child lacks these natural reactions to grief. It is considered a mental disorder when a child cannot recognize signs of anguish and suffering and is oblivious to emotional pain and expressions of sorrow, be it in themselves or others. The grief model, for lack of a better way of saying it, is natural and universal among our species.

The grief model can even be applied to traumatic news that occurred miles from home. When the terrorist attacks of September 11, 2001, played out in front of our gazing eyes, the entire country mourned and went through the stages of grief. We stood in disbelief as the towers fell. We angrily sought immediate revenge on the perpetrators. We wondered if this was preventable and what we could have done to thwart the attack. We cried, and we cried, and we cried. And eventually, we pulled ourselves up by the bootstraps and vowed to move forward as a nation united by tragedy. And, in the sharing stage, we shared the story of 9/11 with our children who were too young to remember it, and we hoped that they would learn something about how sacred every moment of this life really is.

To a further extent, 9/11 gridlocked our professional lives. I know nothing got accomplished that Tuesday in the office where I worked, and little happened for the following few days as portions of our economy were either lagging, locked up, or shut down altogether. I'm sure someone, somewhere, calculated the lost revenues we suffered as a nation due to that day. I can only imagine that the figure is staggering and reached well beyond the events of September 11, 2001, robbing our productivity and profitability for weeks, months, and years afterward.

A community affected by a mass shooting will suffer the same consequences, regardless of whether anyone in their family or their company was lost in the event.

As I noted earlier, selling my mom's house, where memories of my entire life took place, shook me to my very core and was as emotional as the loss of my parents themselves.

Again, a loss is a loss is a loss. And although a loss might be trivial, third-page news to one person, it can be a devastating life-changer to another, and the grief model will play out in some form.

On that note, I close this chapter by emphasizing a critical point. ***The course of grief and the stages of the grieving process are rarely linear.*** People will shift between stages, revert to previous phases, and be tossed around in an ocean of emotions that has its way with their feelings to relentless degrees. This is natural and to be expected. A person may be angry one day and depressed the next, only to revert to bargaining with God and in a state of utter disbelief the following week, and then seemingly making progress through their depression and gaining ground on acceptance, when suddenly they are angry all over again.

Grief is tumultuous and turbulent. It is common for people to be cast about the five stages like a grain of pollen being thrust around by gusts of wind. In my experience, I have found that it is important to recognize the earliest stage that a person expresses, and consider *that* to be the stage they are stuck in. Fleeting moments of anger, bargaining, and disbelief indicate the person is still wrestling with the earliest noticeable stage: disbelief. The ebb and flow of bargaining and depression and moments of acceptance should be considered the earliest noticeable stage: bargaining.

Eventually, stages will drop off almost entirely. At some point, the anger goes away, and the remaining phases are intermingled. Then the bargaining goes away, and the remaining phases are intermingled. This continues until all that is left is acceptance and the person begins to share their experience openly without the need for a box of tissues or a padded room. Sharing their experience during any of the five stages is always good, even if it means the person breaks down into tears when they tell their story. "Letting it out" is always a positive move forward. It should never make you visibly uncomfortable, and you should commend yourself for being someone the grieving person trusts enough to share their story with. Shunning or dissuading someone from sharing their feelings will only exacerbate that person's feelings of isolation, grief, and despair.

As a leader, your primary job is to observe and listen. To be supportive. You need not act upon every expression of grief, although indications of self-harm or self-destructive behavior do require immediate action and intervention. But for the most part, the typical stages of grief only require that you listen and be aware of the person's state of mind. How to adjust your leadership model to cater to that stage of grief will be discussed in future chapters.

The Stages of Grief Chapter Summary

- Know the stages and the characteristics that define them: Denial, Anger, Bargaining, Depression, Acceptance.
- The first two stages of grief can be thought of as the "stunting stages," the next two as the "discovery stages," and then the "growth phase."
- Grieving individuals tend to mask their pain by jumping right to the acceptance phase for the sake of emotional convenience. This is denial, not acceptance. Know the difference.
- The stages of the grieving process are rarely linear. People will shift between stages and even revert to previous phases. This is natural and to be expected.
- As a leader, your primary job is to observe and listen. You need not act upon every expression of grief.

"Funerals seem less about comforting the souls of these dearly departed than about comforting the people they leave behind."

—Rin Chupeco, author
of *The Bone Witch*

CHAPTER 4

Understanding the Funeral Process

*Helping leaders understand how the funeral process and
different cultures mourning practices impact their people*
(Guy Casablanca)

P art of what causes so much stress over someone's loss, no matter the circumstances surrounding their death, is the funeral process itself. It is my job
as a funeral service professional to alleviate the family of that stress and take as
many of their burdens and headaches away as the law will allow. There are some
aspects I am not legally permitted to be involved in, such as affairs of the estate,
life insurance claims, and pending investigation results, but I emphasize to the
families I serve that I am here to take on absolutely anything I can for them.

The very term "undertaker" comes from fulfilling the role of "undertaking"
the duties that the family would not want to be responsible for themselves.
Undertaker, although a term rarely used anymore, is a relatively new moniker. In
the early days of our civilized history, the family handled everything themselves.

Grandma lived in the same house as the generations beneath her. Three
generations of family offspring cared for her up to her death. When she died,
the men would cut the trees and plane the wood to hand-build her casket. The
women would clear the "parlor" of the house (the living area) and pick bunches
of fragrant wildflowers to fill the room and cover the smell of the rapidly decom-

posing body. This is where the term "funeral parlor" came from, and how the tradition of sending flowers to a funeral began.

The family would dress grandma for burial, dig her grave, lower the casket by hand, backfill the grave shovel by shovel, and set a hand-carved tombstone in place. A funeral back then was a lot of work for a family, but there was immense therapy in those tasks. They were not only a labor of love but a means by which to work out any feelings of anger or guilt. There was no way to deny or disbelieve a person's death because you had to deal with the aftermath and do everything yourself in the funeral process. There may be some latent sadness and depression, but relatively speaking, acceptance came quickly. At the end of the extraordinarily laborious and physically demanding funeral process, families were glad it was over and ready to move forward. They had plenty of hours invested in the funeral service and ample amounts of time and energy spent thinking about and processing the loss.

In the modern world, the funeral director and the many industries that service the funeral business "undertake" all those tasks, which alleviates the family's stress on one hand but allows them to avoid dealing with the reality of the situation on the other.

Nonetheless, modern funeral directing provides a remarkable service and makes deliberate efforts to tend to the family's emotional needs as well as honoring things like tradition and ceremony when appropriate, as well as pushing the envelope in novel and creative new ways that are consistent with modern society and the technology available to us. A lot is happening behind the scenes besides the funeral itself, and it is my job to make those things happen seemingly "magically."

But even with all my assistance, a modern funeral is very burdensome on the family. I often liken the task to planning a wedding in three days. A church needs to be booked; an officiant, such as a priest or minister, will need to be scheduled; flowers need to be ordered; music needs to be downloaded; multiple printed materials need to be created, approved, and printed; tribute videos need to be edited and finalized; register books compiled; online announcements posted; newspaper notifications submitted; legal certificates registered and obtained; catering arranged; motorcade escorts scheduled; proper seating decided; additional vehicles obtained; sometimes dove releases, musicians, and other unique accommodations and tributes need to be booked; parking accommodated; attendants and employees committed; the entire service needs orchestrated (without a rehearsal that involves the attendees and key players); webcasting set up; lots of checks cut and accounting done; frankly the list continues ad nauseam. I have only listed the items that overlap with my comparison to a wedding. I have not even addressed the cemetery, the body, and many other elements exclusive to the funeral itself.

I list this cacophony of commitments not to toot my own horn but rather to bring up a valid point. Even though I try to alleviate the family of all these responsibilities and then some, it is very difficult for a family to detach themselves from these concerns. Remember the first day you dropped your kid off at daycare so you could have your own productive time to get things done, and then spent the entire day worrying about their safety, comfort, happiness, and well-being? Grieving families have the same dilemma. They require constant communication and confirmation that everything is coming together as planned and that it's all going to be okay. And it seems like the less conventional funerals suffer the most worry, as there is no standardized set of protocols to follow. A traditional Catholic service, for example, helps provide structure to the chaos of planning a meaningful, memorable, and sentimental life tribute. As modern life seeks to incorporate new ways of memorializing someone, the creative and literal resources required to accomplish that task get more burdensome.

The above paragraphs contain a lot to digest, and this has just scraped the tip of the iceberg in regards to the funeral process. It is important to know what your grieving employee is going through as they try to navigate the often unchartered territory of planning a funeral.

There are essentially three common types of service: traditional funeral with burial, cremation, and devout religious or cultural rituals. As always in the world of grief and loss, there will be variables, subsets, and combinations of these three categories.

Before any funeral service planning begins, the family will be burdened with a few tough and time-sensitive decisions. The immediate obligation is selecting a funeral home. Hopefully, this can be or has been decided before the time of actual need arises, but in cases of unexpected or tragic deaths, it is unlikely that the family will be prepared to make that decision on the fly. They will need to just pick up the phone and start calling around to see which funeral provider can accommodate their service and budgetary needs. Once death has occurred, a hospital or nursing facility will want to discharge and release the deceased as soon as possible. The sooner a decedent comes under the care of a funeral home, the better for everyone involved.

Embalming requires family approval, and although it is a sensitive subject to broach so early in the process of losing someone, it is imperative to the success of a quality viewing of the body to complete the embalming as soon as possible postmortem. I have been involved in many cases where the family is split as to whether a viewing is appropriate. Everyone heals in different ways, and although the spouse might not need a viewing for closure, the sibling of the deceased might well need it to come to terms with the reality of the loss. So before the decedent has even made it from their hospital bed to the morgue, difficult, divisive decisions need to be addressed.

If a coroner is involved in the case of an accidental or a sudden, unattended death, a different kind of stress evolves. Nobody likes to think of their loved one in the cold, clinical environment of a medical examiner's autopsy suite, covered in a sheet and awaiting the invasive procedures of an investigative necropsy. Families want their loved one in a funeral home as soon as possible, but the law will ultimately determine how quickly that can happen. This can be a very stressful time for family members.

Once the deceased arrives at my facility, the stress of "where are they" is generally alleviated, and a certain sense of comfort for the family usually accompanies that moment. I will call the family of the decedent as soon as possible when the body arrives to put their mind at ease and let them know that their loved one is under our watchful eye and in safekeeping. Deliberate word choice and terms that offer a sense of security seem to be most helpful in alleviating a family's concerns about where their loved one is and how they are being treated.

When I make that phone call to inform the family that I have the deceased in our facility, I will schedule a conference for them to come into the funeral home and finalize the service arrangements. At the same time, I send the family a preparatory e-mail that helps to make them aware of the information and items I will need to serve them best, and things I'll need to know to start the legal filings that need to be done at the county level. Hopefully, by the time they arrive for that meeting, they will have a good idea of what kind of funeral they would like.

Traditional funerals with burial, although rife with complex customs of their own, are typically dictated by at least some semblance of ritual that will be handled by the church or religious affiliation. Nondenominational services will require a little more personalized craftsmanship, and completely secular services can pretty much go in any direction the family likes. From my experience, the less religious affiliation, the more oversight and involvement is required on behalf of the family, as they will decide the things that a church or religion normally dictates, and they will do the things the church usually does.

A General Social Survey conducted in 2014[1] revealed a shift of 7.5 million Americans who no longer identified with any religious beliefs since the previous study in 2012. Numbers compiled by the National Funeral Directors Association (NFDA)[2] resonate similar findings. In 2005, 61 percent of Americans opted for traditional funeral services, but by the year 2030, only 21 percent will choose a funeral comprised of traditional elements. For now, the tradition of the funeral ritual inclusive of earthen burial is hanging on by a thread within the Baby Boomer generation, as it was part of their parent's social construct, but it is quickly falling away as cemetery burial comes with its own set of complications, requirements, and costs.

Typically, a cemeterian will accompany the funeral director in the arrangement meeting with the family, as cemetery and funeral services have their own sets of vocabulary and customs, and both require a specialist for the discussion. When both the funeral director and cemeterian are capable, compassionate, competent professionals, the family is put at ease by their expertise and ability to make the process simple. If the cemeterian and the funeral director are incongruent with each other, or even worse, both utterly inept, the family can be scarred by the experience, rather than comforted by the arrangement meeting. I have had firsthand experiences where I have established an extremely amicable rapport with a family, but a personality conflict with the cemeterian completely undid all my progress and left the family with a bad impression of the entire funeral planning process. I have even had full-service funerals with a viewing and burial turn into direct cremations with no services at all due to inconsistent messaging that arose between my funeral arrangement meeting and the cemetery discussions.

Speaking of cremation, it is no mystery or surprise that the popularity of cremation has been increasingly dominating the funeral marketplace for decades. In 2017, the national cremation rate exceeded the 50 percent mark for the first time. This, in part, was aided by the acceptance of cremation by the Christian faiths, most notably the Catholics. Cremation was once considered inconsistent with the Christian belief that the dead would one day be resurrected. If there is no physical, complete body to resurrect, how could one be resurrected? But the pope recently announced that cremation did not conflict with the institution of Christianity so long as the cremated remains were kept together, not scattered, and not partitioned into separate portions. One exception to this ruling has been the Eastern Orthodox religion, which maintained its stance against cremation.

Most assume that the dramatically more affordable nature of cremation has been a prime mover behind the market shift away from traditional funeral services followed by burial, but from an insider's perspective, I see a different reason: convenience and comfort.

Sure, cremation costs less than a traditional burial. It avoids the expense of a casket, a burial plot, a burial vault, cemetery fees, and many of the facility and personnel costs involved with a traditional service. But the main reason I see families opting for cremation is due to convenience, both literal and emotional.

Cremation allows a family to move through the funeral process quickly, with minimal engagement, and few burdening details. They can have the deceased cared for immediately and come back to the idea of a memorial service or life celebration event at a later time, when the emotional stress of the loss has dissipated, and when it is most convenient for everyone to gather for a funeral service or memorialization. Conversely, traditional funerals require very demanding timeliness. Everything has to fall in place perfectly in order to coordinate all the moving parts of a full-blown funeral, and frequently, someone close to the decedent is going to miss the service due to the demands of their job or their life.

But cremation is far more forgiving in the planning and execution of the funeral service. It offers the family more time to plan a tribute that is unique and meaningful. They can schedule the services to meet all the attendees' demanding lives. They can craft and customize with greater clarity. But that only happens about half the time.

The other half of the time, what happens is that the urn is taken home and put on a mantel or in a closet, the family moves through their grief in their own way, and they eventually move on without any fanfare or ceremony whatsoever. By the time they feel ready to plan a life celebration, they do not want to be reminded of the loss, relive the pain, or disturb their emotional state by essentially starting from scratch with funeral planning. Ultimately, what I see most often is the family will "roll" the memorial service into some other function, like a family reunion, graduation dinner, or birthday celebration when everyone will be together anyway. They'll tell a story or two, make a toast to their lost loved one, express their sadness over the fact that the deceased is not there, and that will be the extent of it.

It is a sad testimony to our inherent nature to avoid the things we don't want to deal with. Cremation lends favorably to this phenomenon.

For those who do wish to have a full life celebration or burial of the urn soon after the loss has occurred, the process that accompanies a full-service funeral will be similar but typically more affordable. Make no mistake about it: I have orchestrated memorial services that were far more complicated and expensive than traditional funerals, but those are the exception to the cremation rule. I am in no way trying to shun the option of cremation. Sometimes the simplicity is perfectly appropriate for the wishes of the deceased and the nature of the family dynamic.

What I like about cremation is the ability it gives a company or corporation to hold a memorial celebration of life that incorporates the coworkers of the decedent. It would probably not be appropriate to have casketed remains displayed in a production or manufacturing facility, but putting an urn on display and having a gathering of commemoration is permissible almost anywhere that the deceased left an impression on the world and the people they knew and loved. This is why scattering ceremonies are commonplace. Grandpa's favorite fishin' hole is the best place to hold a memorial service for him, even if it's just the immediate family in attendance.

Considering that about 50 percent of the people who come to funerals are coworkers, the workplace can be the most appropriate place to commemorate that person. It doesn't have to be the primary place for a memorial service, but do not rule out how much the decedent's coworkers may appreciate having the opportunity to honor their fallen friend in the very place their relationship began and grew. Many coworkers have known the deceased for a decade or more but don't know the spouse, family, or other friends of that person and would not feel comfortable going to a funeral or memorial service where they will not know anyone. Asking the spouse or family of a deceased team member if you may hold a memorial tribute to their family member at their place of work, with or without an urn present, sends a clear message of respect and compassion, and nothing less. That gesture speaks volumes about how your organization respects the loss of an employee and how deeply it values any member of the company, no matter their title or position. Do not rule out the emotional value of having a memorial service at work. Since the memorialization event may or may not have an urn or container present, this gesture can follow any type of funeral the family may have had on their own.

Lastly, I'd like to address the funerals of unique cultural customs. Orthodox Jewish faiths, Muslim beliefs, Taoists, and Buddhists all have particular customs that may require you as a leader to accommodate the team member who needs to participate in rituals of culture.

You might not recognize the vice president of sales when he comes to work after his father's Buddhist funeral. If his family is from Laos, he will need to shave his head and walk alongside the temple monks as he personally escorts his father's casket to the crematory and starts the flame generator himself. If he is a Vietnamese Buddhist, he will perform the same ritual, but there will not be a need to shave his head.

The Muslim custom requires, in most cultures, disposal of the body within twenty-four hours of death, and technically it should be returned to the person's native country's earth in that time frame. Although this is rarely accomplishable under the American standards and legal requirements after death, it will be necessary for family members to drop everything and tend to the body of the deceased immediately. As a funeral director, I must allow the family to perform certain rituals of washing and dressing within hours of the person's passing to facilitate their passage into the next life. Your company will need to accommodate the time required for these same rituals.

Hindus also require an especially expedited cremation process. In their belief system, the soul of the departed will be desperately trying to return to their physical body until they are cremated. This is a stressful and troubling ideology that lays large amounts of responsibility on the immediate family. Imagine that your deceased mother would be trying to get back into her own body and take another breath until you personally did something to release her into the afterlife. There is also limited time to return the ashes of the person of Hindu culture to the Ganges River, and believe me, getting a foreign consulate to quickly authorize and allow the urn containing the cremated remains into the person's country of origin is no small task. Likewise, the family of the decedent will be scurrying to find flights that will allow them to be present for that committal into the Ganges.

Orthodox Jews may need to sit Shiva, a mourning ritual spanning seven days and nights. My Jewish clients also participate in bathing and dressing ceremonies that are unique to their culture, and they need to find a cemetery that allows for bottomless grave vaults, as the all-wooden construction of an orthodox casket must be allowed to make direct contact with the earth and return that person to the soil from which they came.

Native American cultures have their own rituals that vary from tribe to tribe, with some aspects universal to all Native American culture.

Just as the funeral process has evolved over centuries from its foundation in the ancient Egyptian practices, where "funerals" are considered to have begun, to the modern-era rites and rituals we attend today, the current methodologies employed in the tradition of commemorating someone's life are accelerating at a record pace. We have not discussed things like "green burial," "human composting," "alkaline hydrolysis" (water cremation), "promession" (cremation by use of liquid nitrogen and the freeze-drying process), burial suits, burial pods, cryonic suspension, and celestial disposition: yes, your cremated remains can now be launched into low-earth orbit to burn up upon re-entry into the earth's atmosphere, or sent beyond the gravitational pull of the earth for a journey through the solar system. Your family can even follow your journey via a memorial hyperlink online that will track your capsule's location through the cosmos, and they can watch a video of the rocket launch that jettisoned you into space.

Interstellar travel aside, as a compassionate and concerned leader, it is important to know the cultural relevance of your bereaved associates and to be ready to accommodate their needs. Being even remotely educated about their customs and rituals shows a level of respect for their beliefs that will put them at ease and communicate a genuine concern for their emotional well- being. If you know an associate is coming into an anticipated death event, start educating yourself on their culture. It will be a pleasant surprise to them that you invested some time and energy with their future needs in mind. It will be a ray of light in their darkest hours.

In summary, the funeral processes of varying types and customs will require your leadership to consider a wide degree of factors. You might have to let someone shave their head, leave the country, or wear a black armband—things that may fall outside the realm of your typical expectations for someone's presentation at work. Know that the planning of a funeral is stressful and only adds to the emotional instability that comes with the loss itself. Often, the grieving process will not even begin until the event of the funeral itself is completely over.

Understanding the Funeral Process Chapter Summary

- Before any funeral service planning begins, the family will be burdened with a few tough and time-sensitive decisions that will affect their state of mind before you may know a loss has occurred.

- Consider that about fifty percent of the people who come to funerals are co-workers. Grief extends far beyond the immediate family, and the chances are strong that your organization has multiple people experiencing some level of grief regularly.

- Take time to educate yourself on the rituals and customs of your cultural colleagues, coworkers, and associates. A good leader who values diversity acknowledges the implications and idiosyncrasies of a person's faith or culture and how they will play out during a time of loss.

- You might have to let someone shave their head, or leave the country, or wear a black armband, as well as other things that may fall outside the realm of your typical expectations for someone's presentation at work.

- Often, the grieving process will not even begin until the event of the funeral itself is completely over or the emotionally traumatic event has had time to register fully.

"Planning is bringing the future into the present so that you can do something about it now."

—Alan Lakein, author of *How to Get Control of Your Time and Your Life*

CHAPTER 5
The Need for Preventive Measures

*Background on how a little planning can help
ease some of the stresses of a loss*
(Guy Casablanca)

The first chapter of this book mentioned an overall goal that we have until now left relatively unmentioned: minimizing the lost productivity and hence the lost profits that grief besieges on your organization and ultimately on the nation's GDP as a whole. Now that we have brought to light various aspects of grief and some of the factors that contribute to and complicate it, we can begin to address what you can do as a compassionate leader to strategically mitigate and minimize the complexities affecting someone who has suffered a significant loss and, eventually, allow them to regain their productivity.

I will touch upon this next topic with a deliberate sense of brevity. This conversation approaches things the law does not allow me to get involved in as a funeral director, so I elaborate on these concepts with the caveat of "from my experience." I am not a lawyer or financial advisor, so do not interpret this chapter as legal or financial advice, but rather as a mere list of suggestions based on what I have witnessed during hundreds of family conferences.

The age-old adage "an ounce of prevention is worth a pound of cure" certainly applies here. Addressing some things ahead of the moment of need will help minimize one's emotional turmoil, if not effectively abolish certain stressors.

In my opinion, as part of a company's total rewards package, an estate planner should be made available to all employees. Many professional estate planners will consult with potential clients for free. Should the employee decide to apply the advice they receive, they can contract with the estate planner to carry out a deliberate course of action.

We tend to assume that if we do not have multiple vacation homes and large investment portfolios, then we don't need the services of an estate planner, but just the opposite is true. People of extravagant means already have advisors who focus on the details of their complex estates, but the average person rarely makes such plans. We believe that our single mortgage on a three-bedroom ranch home, a vehicle or two, and a checking account does not warrant the services of an estate planner. But a professional planner will execute documents that detail what is to happen to those assets in the event of your death. It can be more complicated than you think. When the deliberate assignment of the simplest of assets is not detailed in a legal document, those assets will fall into the realm of probate. Without going into a lengthy conversation about it, I can safely tell you that you do not want your estate, no matter how seemingly small or simplified, to fall into the realm of probate.

Furthermore, an estate planner will address and document your end-of-life wishes, such as having a detailed living will and a DNR ("do not resuscitate") order. This simple decision may prevent your entire life savings and any liquefiable assets you have from being used to pay for your prolonged vegetative state on life support for an indefinite period of time.

The "who gets what" arguments that I see erupt between grieving family members can be precluded or exacerbated by a lack of estate planning. Even if the only item of value that grandma had was her wedding ring, that one object can divide and destroy a family in a matter of minutes, instigating arguments and contentions and grudges that will last a lifetime and splinter the entire family tree. I've seen it happen time and time again.

Advising your associates to consult with an estate planner can circumvent many issues, simple as they may seem, that will become extremely complicated in the event of someone's passing. It's even more unlikely that your associate's grandparents have contracted the services of such a professional. In any event, what could be a very complicated and stressful state of affairs upon death can be minimized into a very cut-and-dried process with the help of even the most basic services of an estate planner. It should almost be mandatory that we all consult with such a professional upon marriage and the bearing of offspring. So much stress—so very much stress—can be avoided by doing so. Furthermore, suggesting to your employees that they consult with an estate planner sends a subliminal message: "I believe you, your time, and your life are valuable and deserve the attention of a professional planner, even if you yourself don't realize just how important you are to your family and our company."

The other common misconception I see over and over is the assumption that a Durable Power of Attorney (DPOA) document is the only item needed to designate someone as the sole authority to make another's final arrangements. It is, for all intents and purposes, worthless once someone dies.

A DPOA ends when the creator's life ends. What it is meant to do is to designate authority to someone to make critical life choices for the person who wrote the document. For example, if I cannot make critical decisions for myself regarding my medical treatments and the money used to pay for them, "Person X" has the authority to make those decisions on my behalf. I am entrusting Person X to carry out my wishes, as expressed within the DPOA document. The document is valid until the time of my death.

Even though it says, in clear print and no uncertain terms that the document ends upon the death of the person who designated it, the person named as having the power of attorney inevitably overlooks that statement, assuming that they have the authority to make the funeral decisions. They do not.

What is really needed is a separate document called a DPOAHC—a Durable Power of Attorney *for Healthcare*. But why?

By the letter of the law, a person's funeral is the last act of healthcare for that person. The DPOAHC carries over, postmortem, to allow the person designated in the document to make both medical and funeral decisions without needing the consent of others, be they family members, spouses, or any other relationship to the deceased.

This decision making authority is crucial, especially when the option of cremation is on the table. If a person's desire is to be cremated, then I, as the funeral director, must receive the consent of either the surviving spouse, a majority of the surviving children, or the parents of the deceased to cremate that person legally. That is the legal hierarchy of authorizations needed: spouse first, or then the surviving adult children, or then the surviving parents (if no spouse or children exist). If there are five children and I can only find two who agree with cremation, then I cannot cremate. I do not have the majority of the children's authorization, meaning that three of the five could legally contest that decision. If there are only two living adult children, I need both their signatures to authorize the cremation. I always need both parents' signatures to authorize the cremation of a child. Even if they are divorced, with one parent having full custody, and a protection or restraining order against the other parent, I still need both parents' authorization.

However, if the holder of a DPOAHC steps forward with a document that expressly communicates the deceased's instruction to be cremated and such wishes are to be carried out by the designee named in the document, then all those other parties' preferences are negated. A DPOAHC carries that much weight.

I have seen many instances where either the decedent knew that they could not trust their offspring to make funeral decisions, or no offspring, parents, or spouses existed, and the decedent did not want their body and funeral to fall under the jurisdiction of the county. Many times, the decedent knew that their children would fight over their estate. In an effort to thwart the most greedy from opting for the cheapest method of final disposition possible, they designated someone outside the family as DPOAHC to handle their final wishes appropriately. The DPOAHC typically does not award the designee the right to inheritance or assets of the deceased but simply gives them the power to make decisions based on the decedent's communicated preferences. When no legal party exists, or no children, no spouse, and no parents come forward to handle the funeral arrangements, the county steps in and ultimately takes jurisdiction over the final disposition. This is also what happens in cases of indigence, when the deceased is either homeless, penniless, or both. A DPOAHC document can avoid this extreme stress before it has a chance to explode.

Another document that can avoid massive amounts of stress is a pre-need funeral plan. Although requiring ample amounts of forethought typically not possessed by most people, a pre-need insurance policy is the highest-ranking document for carrying out one's final wishes.

I wish everyone could witness how smoothly my funeral arrangement meetings unfold when a pre-funded pre-need plan is in place for the deceased. There are no tough decisions to ponder, no hard questions to answer, and no massive bills to take on. A few simple questions, a few signatures, and that's about it. When someone has taken the time to put their final wishes into a legal document that has been underwritten by an insurance company and guaranteed by a funeral provider, there is no room for argument. There is no latitude for divisive controversy, and no need to burden family members with unanticipated expenses. A pre-funded pre-need is the ultimate stress relief for family members. It reduces a three-hour funeral arrangement meeting to thirty minutes or so. It reduces thousands of dollars of expenses to maybe a few hundred dollars, if the family wishes to add a few things to the services that were not covered by the initial policy, such as additional death certificates, flowers, or a motor escort for the funeral procession. It makes the difficult decisions easy. It makes the long processes short. And it makes a world of difference in how quickly the family can move right into their own healthy grieving process without being delayed by the stresses of the final decisions.

Hopefully, you can find a comfortable and effective way to communicate to your staff the importance of addressing these issues before they become emergency priorities. The goal of this book is to offer ways to guide your people into positions of strength and confidence so that they can move forward with as little suffering as possible when someone dies and therefore be more productive when they return to the workforce. The three simple preventive measures outlined above will help aid that cause tremendously.

No document can be prepared in advance that will heal a broken heart in times of unexpected tragedy, but alleviating the stress endured by the funeral planning process will undoubtedly help. Estate planning, DPOAHC, and pre-funded pre-arrangement plans achieve that goal of eliminating a complicated and stressful funeral process.

The Need For Preventive Measures
Chapter Summary

- Consider making an estate planner available to all employees. Estate planning can mean the difference between having to go through probate court or not. You do not want an estate, no matter how seemingly small or simplified, to fall into the realm of probate.

- Encourage the use of Durable Power of Attorney for Healthcare, and know the difference between it and a general Durable Power of Attorney.

- Encouraging your employees to utilize an estate planner and take these preventive measures sends a message that says "I believe you, your time, and your life are valuable and deserve the attention of a professional planner, even if you yourself don't realize just how important you are to your family and to our company."

- Encourage the implementation of Pre-Planned funeral arrangements. This doesn't necessarily mean having your associates buy expensive funeral policies. Just having their loved ones' desired wishes written out and on-file with a funeral provider can alleviate a massive amount of stress.

"I never thought in terms of being a leader. I thought very simply in terms of helping people."

—John Hume, 1998 Nobel
Peace Prize recipient

CHAPTER 6

The Role of Aftercare

*Understanding that you, and your leadership, are
a part of the aftercare process*
(Guy Casablanca)

Some people thrive on chaos and turmoil and perform their best under stressful situations. Others shut down entirely and sleep their way through the roughest of times, usually letting the people mentioned above do all the work. Still others manage to remain as focused as possible on the surface while falling apart on the inside, unbeknownst to the people around them. You will see true strengths and weaknesses revealed when someone experiences the death of a loved one or an emotionally traumatic event. You can forget all your personality profiles, lengthy questionnaires to indicate their character classification, and type A/type B standardizations. None of that will matter when they are stripped of all their defenses, and pure, unfettered emotion takes hold. To that note, I am reminded of a song lyric by the legendary artist Billy Joel:

We all have a face that we hide away forever

And we take them out and show ourselves when everyone has gone.

You might not recognize the person you once knew when they are enveloped in grief. It is unfair to pass judgment on them in this period, yet it is wise to take mental notes. Their innermost vulnerabilities, soft spots, rough edges, and hot buttons will be cresting the surface of their personality under the stressful situation of grief.

So now the funeral is over, a week or so has passed, and the bereaved employee returns to work. This is the time when we funeral directors apply what's called "aftercare." It unfolds during the period immediately following the funeral, when the reality of the situation has time and space to really set in and beat someone down. When appropriate, I try to warn my clients in advance that this period can be the most emotionally challenging.

Until now, there has been a lot of activity demanding the bereaved's attention and energy. They have been running on adrenaline, sleeping in small stints, eating when reminded, and kept in perpetual motion by their primal survival skills and the need to handle all the tasks at hand. Their phone rings incessantly with offers of condolences and questions about circumstances. Their house is bustling with visitors, both anticipated and unannounced. They will be contacted by people they haven't seen or spoken to in years. They will form new relationships with people they just met in the funeral process, and they will rekindle old relationships they had let slip by the wayside of a demanding life. They will laugh as they share stories, cry as they share memories, and experience a cacophony of emotions that spans the full spectrum of the human experience.

And then, suddenly, it's all over. Everyone else goes back to their normal lives. Relatives go back home. The phone stops ringing. The unannounced visits abruptly cease. Food stops coming to the house. Friends get on with their daily routines. All that is left is utter loneliness and a sense of vast emptiness without the person they loved being there anymore. This is the *hard* time. This is when reality hits hard. This is when people need the most attention, and this is unfolding just as they are returning to work.

This is when the reality of life moving on regardless of their grief hits. This is when they need support. This is when they need guidance. This is when they need your active engagement as a leader and the support of their coworkers. How you handle a grieving employee when they first return to work will set the stage for how their struggle with grief will unfold in the workplace. This does not have to take the form of a deliberate investigation to see how someone is doing, and it probably shouldn't come from a position of deep personal inquiry. While some people who have suffered a loss will want to talk about the details, others will not. Often, they will elaborate on their own.

If they are hyper-focused on work and on top of all their tasks, it may be a sign that they are using their job to provide a distraction from their grief and to bring a sense of normalcy back into their lives. This is not necessarily a bad thing. It is important to have things to do that pulls them away from being trapped in their emotions all the time. But it is important to know your people and to recognize someone who is using work as a crutch from their grief, rather than as a healthy aid to get back to a normal life. Was this person always very driven and focused, or is this a new phenomenon?

Conversely, are they constantly checking their social media and neglecting work when they had previously been highly focused? Again, the situational awareness you develop will help you determine if someone is okay or not, grieving in a healthy fashion or not, or just pretending they are okay on the surface. But you will not know any of this without some level of active engagement with that person.

Remember my coworker, whose mother went missing for nine weeks? The leadership at that company did not actively engage that associate. They really did not want to know how she was doing because the mere thought of the potential conversation that could ensue made them uncomfortable. As a result, leadership had no way of knowing that they had a person working on the floor, which, due to her position and mental state, was a liability to the company.

Quite frequently, the first few weeks after a loss is too soon for people to talk openly about what they are going through. They are emotionally vulnerable and may cry at the drop of a hat, and the smallest of things will conjure up feelings of grief. Therapists often refer to this period as "early grief" or "acute grief," and it can last for several months. Remember a tough breakup in your life, when a failed relationship shattered your heart? It probably took months before you could listen to the radio the same way without feeling like you wanted to jump out a window!

The same goes for your grieving employee. If someone in the office wears the same cologne that their departed husband wore, tears will ensue from seemingly nowhere when they catch a whiff of it. Someone else receiving flowers on their birthday can be a reminder that there is no one to send them flowers anymore. The list of potential triggers is endless, as nearly anything can be sentimentalized.

This is natural and to be expected, but it brings up the point that within those first few months after a loss, the bereaved may be at a loss for words regarding their feelings. This is why it is better to check on their *situational* well-being rather than their *personal* well-being. You *know* they are not doing well personally, so see how you can help in other areas of their life as it pertains to work.

About two or three months after a loss, the need to express usually surfaces in even the most stoic of personalities. At our funeral home, we offer free group counseling with a licensed grief therapist every spring and fall. That makes the sessions available to nearly everyone within that two- to three-month period after the death has occurred. I encourage you either to find a group session to recommend or to organize and offer group sessions to your associates when someone in your organization dies, especially if the person who passed had deep connections with the remainder of the organization.

Group therapy is more beneficial than one might first imagine. The impression people have of group counseling usually stems from preconceived notions about twelve-step programs and dependency interventions. That is not how group grief counseling works. There are no badges to earn, no seniority of levels of despair, and no participants who are more experienced than others. You do not attend group grief counseling sessions your whole life as a means of staying un-grieving or as a social support structure to ensure you don't fall back into a state of grief. That's just not how it works.

Rather, everyone is free to speak if they like. Everyone is encouraged to share, and nobody is de-prioritized for not having "lost enough" to have skin in the game. When I speak with people who have attended our grief and loss seminars, they tell me it was surprisingly refreshing, not depressing at all, and they benefitted from hearing other's experiences. They usually feel like they are no longer alone in their grief, and they sometimes realize that their situation is not nearly as bad as it could be—that others have even heavier crosses to bear. It puts things into perspective. And even those enduring the most tragic situations appreciate being around others with a sincere empathy for their plight.

The key is empathy, not sympathy. Empathy is relating to someone's feelings on a personal level, making a conscious effort to truly understand their situation, and not casting judgment, trivializing, or downplaying their emotions and reactions to the circumstances. Sympathy, on the other hand, is more or less being glad it's *them* and not *you* who is going through the grief. Sympathy is typically expressed through sentiments of pity, not genuine concern and understanding. Group counseling offers a setting of an empathetic nature. People there will relate. People there will support. People there will become friends, often to the surprise of the most skeptical attendees.

So now we're a few to several months after a person's loss. To the grief-stricken individual, however, two or three *years* after the loss is a veritable blink of an eye. Years can go by and they are still working through the grief model and grieving process. It is crucial, as a compassionate leader, to recognize that dates of significance will be sometimes subtle, and occasionally not-so-subtle reminders of the loss, and you may see "dips" or regressions in progress when they occur.

Wedding anniversaries, anniversaries of the death, and the holidays are just a few obvious examples. The list of potential significant dates is so vast and varied that it goes beyond what you can anticipate, because many of these significant dates will be well beyond your knowledge. Just know they exist, and try to be understanding of their ramifications. The memory of 9/11 to me is significant, but it is just an ordinary September day to my kids. Dates can be tremendously emotional to some and utterly insignificant to others. Try to be mindful of the fact that these dates will pop up and that grief will rear its ugly, *but healthy* head from time to time even years or decades after the loss. This extends beyond the loss of a loved one. Think of the cancer patient who has to be scanned every three or six months for up to five years. The week or weeks leading up to those scans can be emotionally brutal on them and easily cause them to slip into one or more of the stages of grief until the results are known.

Dealing with people in a state of immense grief on a daily basis has taught me to be very deliberate about my choice of words and phrases. Literally everything I say has the potential to make my job a lot harder and can scar someone permanently. If I do my job correctly and make sure everything I do and say is consistent with the intention of healing and helping, I will serve that family for multiple generations to come whenever someone in their lineage dies. But if I say the wrong thing, fail to choose my words deliberately, or indicate anything less than full empathy and sincerity, I will not only lose the trust of that client but also risk losing future generations to a competitor and potentially scar that person irreparably. Furthermore, they will berate me online, slam our establishment with negative reviews, seek compensation for their suffering, and tell everyone they know just how inconsiderate I was.

What Not to Say

The effectiveness of your leadership will also be subject to intense scrutiny over your communication. In this regard, I offer you the following advice on things *not* to say, as well as what you *can* say to a grieving or emotionally traumatized person, department, division, or organization.

Don't say "at least." Remove these two words from your vocabulary altogether when addressing the bereaved. Examples are: "At least you have your kids … got forty-five years of marriage with them … you're young and can start again/meet somebody/move on … you have your health … are getting treated."

"At least" statements trivialize and diminish the immediate suffering and emotions of the situation. And don't be tempted to replace "at least" phrases with other words that have the same diminishing effect, like "if anything," or "silver linings." All of these catchphrases will work against you, either immediately or subconsciously in the mind of a grieving person.

Do not mention God. Do not say, for example, "It was God's will … God has a plan … God called them to be with Him." It is natural for a deeply emotionally traumatized person to question their faith or to be angry with their God. Do not add fuel to that fire by mentioning God in any way. If they are not questioning their faith already, you risk inspiring them to do so or insulting their beliefs altogether. If they are atheist or agnostic, your spiritual sentiments will appear "preachy." Steer clear of this moral and ethical dilemma and don't mention God—at least not until the grieving person broaches the subject.

Do not offer simple "condolences." It is empty, meaningless, and generic. Our company has a clear policy about *never* using that phrase. It is probably the most canned expression of sympathy that even the person most removed from the situation can throw out there when they feel obligated to at least say *something*. So you offer your condolences … *and?* What is the grieving person supposed to do with that? It doesn't help them heal, it doesn't provide any real assistance, and it is completely impersonal and useless.

Do not say "If there's anything I can do …" This is another sentiment that is utterly void of sincere intention and far too vague to ever be implemented. You know there is nothing you really *can* do, nothing they will *ask* you to do, and nothing you will really *ever* do to ease their pain. Whenever someone at work sees me under the stress of critical deadlines and massive amounts of work, and they say, "Let me know if there's anything I can do," I typically respond by saying, "Yeah, go mow my lawn. I'm not going to get to it today, and I lost my kid in the backyard somewhere under the growth." Without fail, nobody ever goes and mows my lawn.

I'm being facetious with this quip and this analogy, but the point stands. In all reality, I know my coworkers truly mean that I can delegate tasks to them to alleviate my stress, and that they will do whatever I need them to do within the scope of our work. Still, it's the statement "Let me know if I can do anything" that begs for such a tongue-in-cheek response. Do yourself a favor and just don't use that phrase. You'll get a seemingly polite response for your consideration, but the unspoken retort kept to themselves will be, "Yeah, go mow my lawn."

Don't say or imply that "I know what you're going through." Even if you do know, don't indicate that you are somehow authorized to speak on behalf of the grieving person's feelings. Maybe they are secretly glad their angry and abusive aunt is finally gone and not putting the family through misery—so you don't really know what they are going through and just implied that you did. Maybe they are so grief-stricken that they have been contemplating dropping out of society and living amongst the chipmunks in the woods. The fact that you are still an active member of society proves that you don't know exactly what they are going through.

It is easy to fall into this trap by sharing your own grief story as it relates to the person who is going through a loss. Maybe your story is a perfect parallel to theirs in every way, and you just want them to know that they are not alone in their grief and that someone understands them. Your sixth stage of the grieving process, "sharing what you've learned with others," risks being interpreted as trivializing their grief as a commonplace occurrence. It is okay to express that you can *relate,* but you should avoid saying you *know* what they are going through. Believe it or not, this minute difference in your wording can make a monumental difference in their interpretation of your intentions and your sincerity. Saying you "relate" is indicative of interest in their circumstance. Saying you "know" shifts focus to your own story and away from theirs.

Never, ever ask "How are you doing?" It is hard to overstate how inappropriate this question is.

When I greet people who are arriving at a funeral, I am careful not to say "good morning" or "good evening." There is nothing "good" surrounding their attendance at my establishment. They would much rather not have to be there at all. If I say "good morning," it's interpreted as "good for the funeral home." But good for the attendees? Not so much. I prefer just to say "hello." Likewise, "How are you doing?" is like saying, "I'm an idiot who has no clue what pain and suffering are like and I was wondering if you could enlighten me on the topic when you're done crying."

What to Say

Now that we have covered a few things you shouldn't say, let's talk about the things that you can say—things that will be appreciated and acceptable given the circumstances.

You may say what you truly feel: "I was shocked to hear …"; "I'm going to miss them so much"; "I can't imagine what you're going through." Honest sentiments that express your feelings and your inability to comprehend what the bereaved is feeling in this situation are acceptable. These statements must stay within the construct of both believability and acceptability. Exercise caution before just blurting out your feelings, and keep the parameters of your comments tactful, believable, and within the realm of the workplace. People are adept at detecting the thin clank of a counterfeit, and once their lie detector goes off, it is almost impossible to squelch the ringing in their ears every time you speak. Do not embellish your commentary for their sake. The grieving person is quite aware of the truth, as all pretense has already been stripped of them from the suffering they are enduring. They are in no mood for exaggerations.

I use this next comment quite a bit myself, so I can attest to its effectiveness, honesty, and acceptability: "I wish I had magic words to make this all go away for you. I don't. But I want to help by...." This statement is good to follow with specific gestures, because it acknowledges your inability to rectify the situation, but offers your willingness to help in any way possible, rather than offering the generic "If there's anything I can do" statement. Just putting together a list of resources for local handymen, lawn-mowing services, food delivery options, or affordable daycare services can be a big help and an appreciated gesture. Our funeral home offers a specific Aftercare Program that is deliberately designed to help grieving people identify what services they need after the funeral is over and how we can help them with these things. It has been received with the utmost commendations. A workplace could offer a similar program. We will talk more about how this approach can be powerful and productive when the leader "steps in to help" in Chapters 7 and 8.

You may offer terms of legacy such as these: "Jim taught me ..."; "I'll never forget when ..."; "Her contributions to this company ..." We all wish never to be forgotten, and statements that resonate with a person's legacy are usually welcomed, comforting, and acceptable.

As a general rule, don't feel obligated to say too much. The bereaved often need space to process, not reminders of the situation, and the truth of the matter is that there are no words that can provide relief, so don't feel the need to embellish or over-emote on the loss. Sincere gestures speak louder than words and are more likely to be well received.

The Role of Aftercare Chapter Summary

- Active engagement is required by the people closest to the emotionally traumatized, and that includes you as a leader. Check on the person experiencing trauma frequently, but appropriately, and not too often.
- Things NOT to say: "at least" statements, any mention of God, simple "condolence" statements, "If there's anything I can do...", comparative statements like "I know what you're going through," and never, EVER, ask the general question "How are you doing?".

- Things you SHOULD say: "I was shocked to hear / I'm going to miss them so much / I can't imagine what you're going through," specific statements like "I want to help by… (doing this or that)", terms of Legacy: "Jim taught me…I'll never forget when…Her contributions to this company…"

- As a general rule, don't feel obligated to say too much. Sincere gestures speak louder than words and are more likely to be well received.

"The true price of leadership is the willingness to place the needs of others above your own. Great leaders truly care about those they are privileged to lead and understand that the true cost of the leadership privilege comes at the expense of self-interest."

—Simon Sinek, author of *Leaders Eat Last: Why Some Teams Pull Together and Others Don't*

CHAPTER 7

Adapting Your Leadership Approach *

An introduction to the model of Adaptive Leadership and integrating it into your daily leadership
(Anthony Casablanca)

I spent the greater part of my career as an executive for the world's largest funeral service products provider. During my twenty-eight years with them, I had the opportunity to work for one of the best leaders I have ever encountered. At least he was for me. He was always teaching, when he wasn't chewing your ass to help you drive performance. One of the greatest lessons I learned from him was one that he repeatedly reinforced with the leaders in our company. He warned against the desire for managers and leaders to *lead uniformly*. What tends to happen with leaders is they "latch on" to a leadership style they are comfortable with and have used successfully. This style then becomes their go-to leadership style, which they apply to all the people they lead, regardless of the abilities of those individuals. I fell into this trap as a young leader. After attending a leadership seminar, I decided to adopt a highly participative and employee-empowering style. That style made sense to me and fit who I was as a person. At the time, this was not the rewarded leadership style or the culture of the company. Nevertheless, I had great success in building teams and generating results with my style.

Then one day, I had to hire a staff accountant. Being inexperienced in the interview process, I concluded he had all the skills we needed for the role. Six months later, I had to fire him for performance issues. Looking back on that time in my career, I am convinced that part of the problem was that I was managing a somewhat-skilled person who was new to the role and new to the company. He had not yet adapted very well to his new position or the culture of our organization. My mistake was leading him with the same highly participative, highly empowering, highly autonomous leadership style I was using with the rest of my team. I was delegating tasks when I needed to be directing and following up.

Unfortunately, it was a few years down the road before I would learn what I had done wrong. As I matured as a leader, I began to develop my own teachable points of view on leadership. These points of view developed after reading many books and attending many seminars. Only then did I begin to realize that leaders need to meet associates where they are, not where the leader is. I began to realize that there are attributes that leaders need to continually observe and develop in their people. As I reflected on all my training and experiences, it wasn't until some fifteen years later, while being coached by the leader I mentioned above, that I would be able to put a label on my actions from years past. I was leading uniformly! I was not adapting my leadership style to meet the developmental needs of my team members. I was not observing, as keenly as I should have been, the characteristics and behaviors of my people close enough to allow me to be sensitive to the type of leadership they needed from me.

Let's explore what I am talking about in a little more depth. Several traits can determine the leadership relationship between a leader and a subordinate. While the list can be long, I am going to focus on a few select traits that I believe both drive an employee's performance and indicate how a leader should lead them. The characteristics we will focus on are stewardship, trust, empowerment, collaboration, and communication frequency. I would define these as follows.

Stewardship is the level of ownership, accountability, and competence an employee demonstrates in completing assignments. Generally, people who demonstrate a high degree of stewardship also tend to drive results. People who are stewards of their role or their assigned tasks take it upon themselves to make sure they are learning, growing, and developing their competence in their role. Stewardship is earned through the demonstration of these skills.

Trust is the belief in a person's skills, abilities, integrity, and character. When an employee demonstrates a high degree of this combination of attributes, the leader develops a high degree of trust in that person. Trust is a natural outcome of demonstrated stewardship.

Empowerment is the amount of authority a leader is willing to "give" to an individual to complete a task. Employees who are empowered have naturally demonstrated stewardship and have earned the trust of their leader. Empowerment is where the leader transcends from dictating the "what, why, and how" of an assignment, to reaching an agreement with the employee on what the desired outcome of a task or assignment should be, and then allowing the employee to determine the "how."

Collaboration is the level of sharing information and decision-making authority the leader conducts with an employee. Collaboration is high when the elements of stewardship, trust, and empowerment are present. Collaboration takes place when the leader not only shares the requisite information but also solicits the input of the person they are leading to determine what success would look like and what the desired outcomes should be.

Communication frequency is the cadence required for follow-up, course correction, and approval. Communication frequency is inversely proportionate to the amount of stewardship, trust, empowerment, and collaboration the employee has earned in the relationship. When those elements are high, the communication frequency can be low. When those elements are lacking, then the communication frequency needs to be high.

At this point, many of you might identify additional traits that determine an employee's ability—things like results orientation, problem-solving strength, learning agility, or teamwork, to name a few. I agree with you. However, I would argue that those skills all roll up to determine where you would rate your employees within each of the defined characteristics. If an employee doesn't demonstrate a results orientation, learning agility, or problem-solving ability, you likely will rate them low on the stewardship scale.

Whether your organization's talent management process evaluates skills and abilities, performance and potential, or what and how, or whether it is task-based or competency-based, it will not matter, because what we are going to talk about in the rest of this chapter applies to all these frameworks. In fact, what we will discuss moving forward are principles that are not limited to just leading a grieving employee. They are principles that should be applied broadly and consistently.

As I mentioned earlier, the real secret to avoiding the trap of leading uniformly is being skilled as a leader in determining each associate's development level. Again, whatever performance and talent management system your organization uses will not matter. In every instance, those systems all measure two basic factors. Sometimes they are called "skill and will." Sometimes "what and how." Sometimes "performance and potential." Whatever the labels used, the bottom line is that your people fall on these scales in different places, and where they fall is linked to their developmental level within each of the five elements of stewardship, trust, empowerment, collaboration, and communication frequency. Because of this, they cannot and should not be led uniformly. As a leader, you are therefore faced with a choice. Either you can demand that your associates change their behavior, and all get in the same "block" in the matrix. Or you can adapt your style to meet your associates where they are and help them develop under your leadership to move up and across the matrix.

Let's assume you have reached out to your HR leader to seek some coaching on how to lead your team more effectively. Like me, you have sensed something is not quite right, and you would like to discuss leadership in general and leading your team specifically. Your HR leader asked you to fill out a typical nine-block matrix of your people. She has asked you to plot your team on the matrix, measuring their performance and potential level. Keep in mind that we could easily change "performance" to "skill" or the "what." Likewise, we could change "potential" in this matrix to "will" or "how."

You provide her with the following completed matrix.

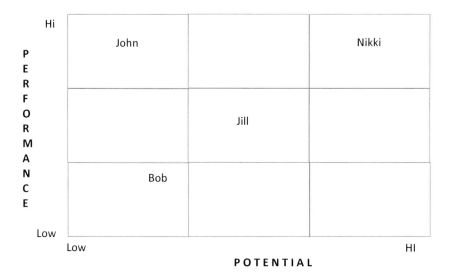

When you meet with your HR leader, she asks you to describe how you lead. You make sure to use all the right buzzwords in your response. You tell her you are an "actions/results-oriented" leader who is very focused on setting goals and achieving them. You also tell her that you are a "communicative" leader who talks to your team a great deal. You are an "effective delegator" who believes the best way to develop your people is to "stretch" them, and that previous leadership assessments have also indicated you are a "decision maker" who is very confident and persuasive.

Your HR leader then shifts the discussion to your team. She says, "Tell me about Bob." You tell her that Bob is relatively new in his role and to the organization. Bob has demonstrated some skill, but in many aspects of his role, he has not yet fully developed. Bob tends to ask a lot of questions and seems uncomfortable when given new tasks or assignments. Bob is still growing in his role, but you believe he has some potential to advance given time and the right development plan and leadership. After asking a couple more questions about Bob, your HR leader says, "Tell me about Jill."

Jill, you say, has been in her role for almost a year. She has been with the company for five years and is a strong player. She was placed in the position to develop specific skills, and she has developed well, meeting all expectations and exceeding some. She has a great attitude, is willing to help others on the team, and, given another twelve to eighteen months of continued development, will be ready for another assignment at that time. Your HR leader agrees with your assessment. She then asks about John.

You tell her John is an interesting case. He is highly skilled in his role. As your most senior person, he has been with the company for fifteen years and has spent the last seven years in this role. You tell her there is no task you cannot give to John that he can't handle. John is a typical high performer. You can give him any task and it will be done with excellence and no surprises. John, however, lacks either the motivation, the confidence, or simply the desire to do more than his current role. After listening to your discussion regarding John, your HR leader asks you to tell her about Nikki.

You tell her that while Nikki has not been with the company or in her role for nearly as long as John, she has excellent learning agility. That agility has allowed her to come up the experience curve quickly and master her role. While her skill level is as high as John's, her potential to take on more responsibilities and more significant roles is far superior. She has a great attitude, takes feedback and coaching well, and wants to advance for the right reasons.

The discussion then returns to how you lead and what has caused you to ask for this meeting. Your response surprises even you. You tell your HR leader that the team doesn't seem to be hitting on all cylinders. Bob and Jill appear to be doing well, but Bob seems to ask repeatedly for guidance, and Jill seems to get frustrated when meeting with you to discuss her progress on assignments. Nikki, on the other hand, is constantly "running off the ranch" in your eyes. She always is looking for more freedom, decision-making authority, and autonomy. You also tell her that you even struggle a bit with John. Sometimes you seem to be on the same page, and other times he, too, seems frustrated.

As the discussion continues, your HR leader begins to explore your description of your leadership style in more depth. As you talk, it becomes clear that what you believe is delegating is really directing, and what you think is superior communication is really persuasion and passive assertion of dominance. It's a startling moment for you, as it was for me when I had similar discussions with my HR leader.

Then the true value of your HR leader comes through. She says, "Let's explore this a little deeper, starting with Bob." Bob is relatively new in his role. Based on your description, he is still coming up the skill curve and is unsure of himself. She asks you how you would rate Bob on the five characteristics of stewardship, trust, empowerment, collaboration, and communication frequency. After a brief discussion of definitions, you respond with the following assessment of Bob. You articulate that, because of Bob's lack of company and job knowledge, you would rate him very low in the stewardship category. As a result, you cannot trust him to get the results required in the time allotted. As you continue the assessment, you tell your HR leader that you do not feel you can empower Bob, and collaborating with him on outcomes would not make sense. You conclude with stating that he likely needs a great deal of communication and follow-up.

Neither of you can believe that you have already used up the two-hour time slot you both set aside to have this discussion. Before ending the meeting, your HR leader asks that you complete an assessment of each of the four members of your team against the five elements discussed based on their skills and needs. Your head is spinning, and you are disappointed that you are leaving the meeting feeling a bit unfulfilled. However, you agree to come back in a couple of days to further the discussion.

You return to your office and go to work on the assessment. After several false starts, you assemble the following chart.

	Bob	Jill	John	Nikki
Stewardship	Very Low	Low to Moderate	Moderate to High	High
Trust	Very Low	Low to Moderate	Moderate to High	High
Empowerment	Very Low	Low to Moderate	Moderate to High	High
Collaboration	Very Low	Low to Moderate	Moderate	High
Communication Frequency	Very High	High	Moderate	Low

A couple of days later, you return to her office to continue the discussion, chart in hand. You spend the first half of the meeting just discussing this chart and ensuring you both understand what each assessment for each person means. She goes on to say that she believes your leadership style of directing and repeatedly following up is likely precisely the leadership that Bob needs. She also cautions you that as Bob continues to develop, he will need you to adapt your leadership style to ensure he continues to grow. You ask what it means to adapt your leadership style.

"Great question," your HR leader says, but she moves on to talk about Jill without providing an answer. You rated Jill higher on all five of the attributes except communication frequency. Based on where her skill level is, Jill likely will respond and perform better if you begin to involve her in the task/assignment development process. While you still need to direct her, she also will need you to explain decisions and expectations to her to enable her to understand better why you are asking her to complete the task and what needs to be done. While you will ultimately be the decision maker, Jill likely would respond well to being asked for suggestions and input in the process. In this way, you will not only be developing her skill level but her future potential as well. In short, because Jill is coming up the trust, stewardship, and empowerment curve, what Jill wants and needs is for you to begin to collaborate with her more. While you fear the extra time and effort it might take to lead her in this manner, you continue to listen.

The HR leader says, "Now for John." John is a high performer by your description, and the rest of the organization would agree. However, since John has such a high skill level, if you direct him on every task and don't involve him in the process of determining the deliverables and the path forward, he will get frustrated. John will feel like you are acting more like his parent than his leader. The tricky thing about John is that in some tasks his skill level is likely very high, while on other assignments, particularly those that are new to him, he may not be as capable and may be a bit more tentative. While John has the skills, he might not be able to see how those skills translate to the particular assignment you have given him. In those instances, he is going to behave more like Jill than Nikki. When this occurs, he will need you to be a bit more involved. When John needs your help and guidance, it will likely come through an open and honest dialogue—a collaborative approach of give and take. Through such a discussion,

John will see for himself how his skills and abilities align with the assignment. He will leave the discussion more confident and with a vision of a successful outcome that he will have shaped himself. While these discussions will likely be an infrequent occurrence, you will need to be aware of when to step in and when to simply collaborate with him and help him see how his skills are right for the job. You think to yourself, *Wow. This is getting complicated.* Then you realize you just said that out loud.

Lastly, the HR leader's attention turns to Nikki. You think, *My style has to work with Nikki.* After all, you think you are a delegator. Your HR leader says, "Now, Nikki is a high-performing, high-potential worker. She has both the skill and the will to take on greater and greater responsibilities and tasks. However, because she rates high on the stewardship, trust, and empowerment scale, she gets her greatest sense of value from being involved in all aspects of the decisions surrounding the task. You call it 'running off the ranch,' but Nikki calls it names like 'trust,' 'responsibility,' 'empowerment,' and 'autonomy.' With Nikki you want to truly delegate—not just assign tasks, which is really directing. There is a vast difference. When you direct, you retain all the decision making and authority in the process of task completion. When you truly delegate, you, as the leader, turn the decision-making process over to the associate. To Nikki, in this case. While it is not abdication, it is highly participative, highly engaging, and highly trusted leadership. With people like Nikki, your role needs to be one of helping her demonstrate her stewardship of the assignments. At the outset, the communication frequency will be high with Nikki. However, once you reach an agreement, that frequency can be significantly reduced. In fact, you may even let Nikki dictate the frequency of communication." You admit you have a great deal to absorb and think about as you leave her office.

Over the coming days you redraw your talent matrix and attempt to add the key points of the discussion with your HR leader. Your new graphic looks something like this.

Hi		Stewardship	Moderate	JOHN	Moderate to HI		HI	Nikki	
		Trust	Moderate		Moderate to HI		HI		
P		Empowerment	Moderate		Moderate to HI		HI		
E		Collaboration	Moderate		Moderate to HI		HI		
R		Communication Frequency	Moderate		Moderate to Low		Low		
F		Stewardship	Low		Low to Moderate		Moderate		
O		Trust	Low		Low to Moderate	Jill	Moderate		
R		Empowerment	Low		Low To Moderate		Moderate		
M		Collaboration	Low		Low To Moderate		Moderate		
A		Communication Frequency	High		High		High		
N		Stewardship	Very Low	BOB	Very Low		Very Low to Low		
C		Trust	Very Low		Very Low		Very Low to Low		
E		Empowerment	Very Low		Very Low		Very Low to Low		
	Low	Collaboration	Very Low		Very Low		Very Low to Low		
		Communication Frequency	Very High		Very High		Very High		

Low   **HI**

P O T E N T I A L

As time passes, you implement the principles your HR leader shared with you. You increase your communication frequency and follow-up opportunities with Bob, and his performance continues to improve. You begin to recognize the instances where John needs more of your input, and you get more involved during those times. You begin to share more of the decision making with Jill, demonstrating that you recognize that the stewardship of her role has grown, and with it, so has your trust in her. Finally, with Nikki, you begin to truly collaborate with her, sharing all the information you can and then some, transforming her "running off the ranch" to harnessed passion and energy that get results beyond your expectations. Things are going well by all measures.

About eight months have passed since your discussion with your HR leader. Nikki comes to your office with a panicked look on her face and tears in her eyes. You say, "Come in and sit down." Nikki says, "I have to leave *now*! I have to get to the hospital. My husband has been in a horrible accident." You ask if she needs you to drive her. She says no. Over the coming days, the information is sketchy. Nikki's husband, Mark, was in a terrible car accident in a freeway construction zone. He was behind a stopped semi with two other cars behind him, all stopped for the construction. A second semi came over the hill and could not stop in time. It hit the last car in line, pushing all three vehicles into a mangled mess. Mark's car was pushed under the semi. His injuries were life threatening, and he died shortly after Nikki arrived at the hospital. It was truly a sudden and unexplainable tragedy. As your team learns of what happened, they are in shock and disbelief. They can't even imagine what is going through Nikki's mind. In the blink of an eye, she has become a widow with two young children. Not much work gets done for the rest of the week.

You decide to talk to your HR leader about the situation. You want to know what you can do to help, what benefit information you can share, and what flexibility you have as her leader to give Nikki time off work. You haven't even thought about the workload Nikki is leaving behind yet. She had been selected to lead an acquisition integration project because of her unique ability to connect the finance world with the IT world and to evaluate business processes to help determine the acquisition's value and potential synergies.

As your HR leader shares the company policies, you learn that your company is like most. By policy, Nikki is entitled to three days of funeral leave for a direct family member. If she wants more time off, she will have to use vacation time. *Three days?* you think. *How is that at all reasonable? She just lost her husband. There is no way I could return to work in three days if I lost my wife.* Your HR leader can see the disgust on your face. She then asks what you will do about the acquisition integration project. You say you are not sure. Nikki's skills are required for the project. While others could help, the project will undoubtedly be slowed. Milestones will be missed, and frankly the acquisition could be at risk. Your HR leader suggests you take a day or so to think things over and schedules a time to meet with you again in a couple of days. Before you leave, she asks, "Do you have any idea what Nikki will be going through?" You say it is unimaginable to you. In an unusually vulnerable moment for her, your HR leader asks you to take a seat and begins to tell you a story from her past.

She says that about five years ago, before being promoted to her current role, she went through an ugly divorce. Her husband had walked out on her and ran off with a younger woman, leaving her with two young children to raise. She said she was devastated. For months she came to work in a fog. She couldn't concentrate. She made mistakes that she would never have made previously. She had to take calls from lawyers during the day. As she sat in meetings, anger would boil up inside her until it could no longer be contained. Then she would snap at the slightest thing and explode on her colleagues. Then there was the crying—not just at home, although there was plenty of that, but here in the office as well. Her boss at the time was never able to understand. "Frankly, he didn't seem to want to know what I was going through," she said. "He continued to expect more from me, and my performance slipped. It slipped to the point that I was put on a performance improvement plan. Frankly, I thought about leaving the company. I recall one mistake I made during a union negotiation. I was responsible for calculating the cost of a fairly complex union proposal. I made an error on my spreadsheet that greatly underestimated the cost by a million dollars. Thankfully, the lead spokesperson questioned the calculation, saying it didn't seem to make sense, and another member of the team found the error. I tell you all this because this is nothing compared to what Nikki will feel when she comes back to work. In addition to dealing with her grief, Nikki will be dealing with two young kids who won't understand what happened to their father. She will be dealing with having to pay all the bills without her husband's income. She will have to deal with navigating benefits and estate laws. She will have to deal with all the reminders of her loss that are all around her, every minute of every day. Let's talk again tomorrow about how you will handle this situation. Bring your talent matrix with you."

Adaptive Leadership Chapter Summary

- One of the biggest leadership challenges is to overcome the desire to lead uniformly.
- Five traits determine the relationship between a leader and a subordinate; stewardship, trust, empowerment, collaboration, and communication frequency.
- An employee's demonstration of these traits can range from very low to very high.
- Overlaying these traits on a performance/potential talent nine-block matrix enables the leader to determine where each employee is in their development cycle.
- Adaptive leadership is learning to adapt your leadership style to match where the employee is in their development cycle.
- Applying adaptive leadership principles and processes will improve the performance of the entire team.

"It is not enough to be compassionate. You must act."

—Dalai Lama

CHAPTER 8
The Art of Leading Grieving Employees *

Learning to use the Adaptive Leadership model to help grieving / emotionally traumatized employees excel at work
(Anthony Casablanca)

Tomorrow comes much too quickly. You grab your talent matrix and your cup of coffee and head to your HR leader's office. Before the "workload" discussion gets started, the HR leader says, "Are you and your team going to the funeral?" You were not expecting that question. You say that your team has talked about it, but you can't shut the entire department down for an afternoon. You also say that you won't know anyone attending the funeral except Nikki, and that you will feel awkward attending. You are also thinking that you have no idea what to say to Nikki and would prefer to put that moment off for as long as possible.

Your HR leader advises you to reconsider your position on attending. She says that Nikki and the entire team will be watching to see how you, as a leader, and the company responds to this tragedy. She also says that Nikki doesn't expect you to "say" anything. Just being there will say enough to her. As for the department shutting down for a day, you will get whatever you believe will be lost productivity from that time back many times over as a result of the discretionary effort your team will put in when they get back. Being allowed to grieve with Nikki will help them bond as a team, and they will work to ensure nothing falls through the cracks as a result of the compassion and understanding you will have demonstrated by your decision.

On the other hand, if you do not attend or allow the staff to attend, you will drive a wedge into your team. It will be a subtle wedge, but it will be there nonetheless. Your team will remember that you lacked compassion when Nikki and the team needed it most, and it will chip away at their loyalty and engagement.

The discussion then turns to the workload and Nikki's mental state when she returns to work. The HR leader begins to ask you questions regarding how Nikki's stewardship, trust, empowerment, collaboration, and communication frequency will likely be impacted by her having to deal with grieving. Again, you think to yourself, *I can't even imagine.*

As you look at your matrix, your HR leader takes it from you and draws three arrows on it and hands it back to you. She says, in short, that when people are feeling the unbearable impacts of grief, their performance will move down and to the left on the matrix. This movement, in turn, will mean that you will have to adjust your leadership style. You will have to do this for sure with Nikki, but possibly also with your entire team for some time. For Nikki, it may take months or even a year before she is back to her previous level in this graphic. For the rest of your team, it will not take that long. She hands you back the matrix, and it looks like this.

The Impact Grief Can Have On An Employee's Performance and Potential

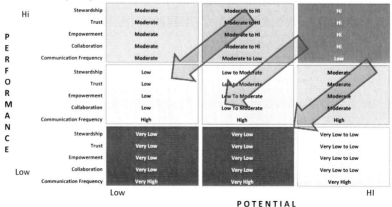

As you talk, you ask the HR leader if you should wait for Nikki to ask for help or if you should ask her if she needs help. She says, "Neither." This paradox is perplexing to you. "How can I do neither?" you ask. Unfortunately, the HR leader explains, one of the unintended consequences of our "high-performance" culture is that people have been conditioned not to ask for help. Our people believe that asking for help is a sign of weakness, and it will be held against them. So, unless Nikki has an incredible amount of trust in you or in HR, she will probably never ask for help or tell you she needs help.

Your HR leader explains that you, as the leader, will need to develop a proactive plan to remove some of the stress from Nikki without making her feel like you are penalizing her or threatening her job. Then you need to discuss the plan with Nikki. Let her know how valuable she is, how involved you want her, and how much the company wants to help her excel at work as she navigates her loss. You ask the HR leader for advice on how to begin this discussion. She advises you to use some version of the following phrase: "I wish I had magic words to make this all go away for you. I don't. But I do want to help by giving you added support and flexibility here at work. Here is what I am thinking …" Then she hands you a book by two authors you had never heard of before. The title is catchy, though: *The Dying Art of Leadership: How Leaders Can Help Grieving Employees Excel at Work.*

You might now be thinking, "That's a touching and heart-wrenching story, but it's made up." However, it is not. During my time as a head of human resources, that very scenario played out for the young wife of one of our salespeople. While she did not work for us, she did have to return to work for her company after her husband was tragically killed. Let's talk some more about the reality of our world and the impact on work environments.

It's August 2019 as we write this, and there have already been twenty-seven mass shootings in the United States since the year began. That's more than all the mass shootings in 2018. What if one of the fathers, mothers, brothers, sisters, or spouses of those killed worked for you? If you work for most of the companies in our country, those people will be expected to return to work within three to five days. Where do you suppose their heads will be when they return?

Or how about this. The spouse of someone who just committed suicide, died of a sudden heart attack, or has suffered a debilitating stroke works for you. How will you deal with them when they return to work?

Or maybe one of your top-performing salespeople calls you in the middle of the night and, with a quivering voice, says his child has just been killed in a horrific car accident. His final words to you are, "I don't know when I will be back."

Or one of your employees calls and says his opioid-addicted son is missing. The fear and panic in his voice is palpable as he struggles to hold back his tears. A cold chill runs down your spine as you realize you had no idea he was dealing with a son who had an addiction problem.

All these examples lead you to the same place. Every one of these people will be returning to work, and they will be hurting deep down inside and grieving. No matter how much they want to return to normal, they will not truly be themselves until they have gone through the five stages of grief. They will do this in their own way, in their own time. They will not be functioning normally until they reach the acceptance phase, and that is a long way from where they are when they return to work. If they appear normal upon their return, they may actually be exhibiting a symptom of denial. One thing will be for certain: they will be emotional and distracted. While I think three days is an absurdly short bereavement policy, this is not a plea for your company to change its bereavement policies. I don't care how much time you give someone to return to work. If they are Nikki, or one of the people in the above examples, no amount of time will be enough. And these examples don't begin to cover the spectrum of events that can cause people to grieve. Maybe your employee has just been told they have cancer that is treatable but very serious, requiring chemotherapy or possibly other treatments. Do you think they are concentrating on the job even if they can come to work in between treatments?

Sheryl Sandberg, chief operating officer of Facebook, wrote a book entitled *Option B*[1]. If you have not read the book or do not know her story, Sheryl lost her husband and love of her life when they were in the prime of their lives. They were on vacation at a resort in Mexico when he collapsed and died during a workout in the resort spa. When he did not show up for dinner, Sheryl went looking for him and found him lying on the gym floor, dead. Here are some of the phrases she uses to describe her return to work: "a complete haze," "everything felt unfamiliar," "why on earth does any of this even matter?," "I actually fell asleep in a meeting." She goes on to say: "Grief felt like a deep, thick fog that constantly surrounded me."

Unfortunately, grief cannot be compartmentalized. Grief is pervasive. To the grieving person, grief is present in absolutely every aspect of their lives. There is no escape from the pain, the hurt, the loneliness, and sometimes the guilt. Additionally, grief feels permanent. It feels like it will never go away, like life will never return to normal. In many respects, this is literally quite true. Grief actually never does go away, and life never does return to what was normal before the loss. It can't. Over time, however, the grieving person's mind learns to adapt to the new normal, and slowly, very slowly, glimpses of joy begin to return.

One thing I can assure you is that the way you, as the leader, handle these folks and their situations will make all the difference in the world. It will make a difference in how they feel about your company. It will make a difference in how they feel about working for you. It will make a difference in how much productivity is impacted by the events. It will make a difference in how your entire team views you and the company. Let me give you two very real examples.

The first takes place in 1989. An acting plant manager at the company's largest manufacturing facility gets a call after driving home from an Easter weekend with his parents and younger brother. After driving home for seven hours, he and his wife get their toddler to bed, and they settle in for the night. They are headed to bed when the phone rings. The voice on the other end is his teenage brother, who says, "I think dad is having a stroke." Over the next thirty-one days, things go from bad to worse. The stroke, it turns out, was caused by a blood clot that broke loose from his father's cancer engulfed pancreas. In thirty-one days, his father is dead at the age of fifty-three, and his mother now has to figure out how she is going to keep the house and survive on literally no money.

The president of the company is aware of what has transpired. For the next several months, a man who had thrown the acting plant manager out of meetings and told him he was not competent, using very colorful words, would call him every week and ask how he was doing. What support did he need? Was there anything the company could do to help with the situation? He told the plant manager to not worry about taking the time he needed to travel back and forth to help care for his mother. He also made arrangements to have the vice president of manufacturing spend more time in the facility to ensure the plant manager didn't feel undue pressure to keep the place running.

That acting plant manager was me. I was twenty-eight years old and spent the next three months traveling back and forth between Manchester, Tennessee, and Dayton, Ohio. Every time I passed the hospital where my father had died, I would cry. Thankfully, I had an incredibly supportive wife to help me through this time. She understood my emotional roller coaster and supported me in taking responsibility for helping my mother figure out her future. However, had the president of the company not done what he did, the pressure I would have felt would have been devastating. I would have felt torn between worrying about keeping my livelihood and caring for my mother. How do you choose between those two things? This was a man, a leader who understood the concepts discussed in the previous chapter and what will be discussed later in this one.

Here is a contrasting example. The president of an operating division is on vacation in northern Michigan with his wife. It was late May in 2014, and they are enjoying the scenic drives along Lake Michigan and just relaxing. They are checking emails and voice mails once or twice a day, but for the most part they are decompressing. On the morning of June 1st, he gets a call from his grandmother's nursing home. His ninety-eight-year-old grandmother has passed away during the night. His routine of checking voice mails in the morning is now disrupted by the need to call family members and inform them of the loss and trying to make funeral arrangements from hundreds of miles away.

While there is a surviving daughter, she lives in New York, a thousand miles away. So, kind of by default, our lead character in this story inherited the responsibility for his grandmother when his mother passed away in 2010, four years earlier. He cuts his vacation short, drives his motorcoach home, and uses the rest of his vacation planning the funeral and cleaning up what he can of his grandmother's estate. When he returns to work, things are fine. His grandmother's death was no surprise. She had stopped eating a couple of months earlier, and before he left on vacation she asked him, "When is the funeral director coming to get me?" She was ready to be with her husband, her daughter, and her brothers. The president's grieving process was fast, almost moving right to acceptance skipping all the other steps. Not uncommon for this type of situation. When he returns to work after the funeral, his boss, the vice president of the operating division, calls him and says, "You take a lot of time off work!" He said this even though he knew that this was a two-week approved vacation, the last week of which was spent primarily on funeral leave. Which of these leaders would you rather work for? Which of these leaders would cause you to be even more engaged and more loyal? Which of these leaders would make you feel proud of the company you worked for?

I am the central figure in this vignette as well. I can tell you, hands down, I would take all the verbal abuse and criticism of the first leader any day and would work for him again based on the way he handled the death of my father in 1989. As for the second person? I still have a hard time thinking of him as any type of a leader. This treatment also sent a clear message to me about how the culture of the company where I had worked for thirty-one years was changing, and not for the better.

The point of these two stories is simply to demonstrate that what you do at these critical times in your employees' lives, and how you chose to lead, matters! It's not just business as usual for an employee stricken by grief. What you do matters to them and to the rest of the organization, and it affects the productivity and performance of your team, function, department, and possibly even the entire organization, depending on the circumstances. The grips of grief are distracting at best and debilitating at worst for the grieving individual. As we discussed in earlier chapters, while everyone moves through all five stages of grief in every situation, how long each stage takes to get through and the duration of the entire process depends on the type of loss, the situation of the loss, and the closeness of the relationship impacted by the loss. Hopefully, you, as the leader, are close enough to your people to be able to understand and explore each employee's situation. If you are not, there are many other books you should be reading and seminars you should be attending in addition to this one!

How exactly does grief impact the workplace? One of the most vivid interpretations of grief I have seen is by artist Celeste Roberge. She sculpted a human figure on its knees crumbling under the weight of thousands of rocks. The sculpture is called *Rising Cairn*, and is often referred to as "The Weight of Grief."[2]

I have experienced this weight in my own life, and I have witnessed it more times than I care to in the lives of people I have led. What this means to you as a leader is that you have to be present. It means that you have to be willing to lead in the uncomfortable moment. It means you have to care and be willing to let your people know you care. It means you have to communicate and direct your team more. As we illustrated in the matrix we discussed in the previous chapter, when an employee is working through the five stages of grief, they will naturally slide down and to the left on the matrix. Some may move a great deal while others move only slightly, but they will move. This shift will be true for everyone except for the person who is already in the lower-left corner who has nowhere else to move. The result of this movement is that you will be required to communicate and lead the impacted employee more than previously required. Even the person in the lower-left corner who was already receiving heavy direction is going to need more support from you. It means you are going to have to master the art of leadership, adapting your leadership style to fit where this grieving, hurting employee currently is, through no fault or choice of their own. They are not the same person you knew when they last left the office.

You may be wondering how an employee's potential can be impacted by grief. If they had exhibited high potential before the loss occurred, how can they have lost it? Stated another way, if they had the skill and will to advance before the loss, how could that change? Let me give you some examples.

Your employee's father dies at age seventy-five, leaving his spouse, your employee's mother of a similar age and in failing health, to take care of herself. Your employee feels compelled, rightfully so, to "put their career on hold" to stay close to their mother. As a result, your employee is no longer willing to relocate or travel as much as they previously had. Over the next few years, that employee is no longer on the high-potential list because they cannot relocate for the next developmental assignment. I was in that position after our mother passed away in 2010 when I became responsible for our ninety-four-year-old grandmother's care. The president of the company I worked for asked me if I would be willing to relocate overseas to take a developmental assignment. I had to decline. Fortunately, this was the same president who preached about not managing uniformly, and he understood that I needed support during this time in my life. My declining the opportunity was not looked upon as a black mark or a strike against me. Quite the contrary. He used the opportunity to explore what was going on in my life. We talked about how I had just relocated my grandmother from Dayton, Ohio, to an assisted-living facility literally in the back yard of our corporate offices. As a result, I was unwilling to move five thousand miles away and leave her all alone. He assured me the company would look for other opportunities for me. Three years later I was named president of an operating company in Cincinnati, Ohio, an easy forty-five-minute commute from my home. As you read about this example, think about the stresses this situation would put on your employee. Not only are they grieving the loss of their loved one, but they are also feeling the weight of needing to care for their mother (grandmother in my case), and now they are also worried about their career. That is a lot of rocks to be carrying around, and those are merely the obvious ones.

While the impact of grief on an employee's performance may be more obvious, let me give you another example of trauma that I experienced many years ago when I was a new leader in a trucking company. The phone rang. I answered it, and one of our drivers told me, "I just killed someone with my truck." His voice was stoic, and it was clear he was in shock. Having to balance compassion for him with the need to start documenting what happened, I asked him for details. I could hear the quivering in his voice as he explained that a car swerved and crossed the median on this rainy, foggy night. It was about dusk when this happened. The vehicle struck him head-on. It all happened so fast he could not have reacted. Our driver was not cited. We sent people up to get him and drive him home, and we had the truck towed. When he got back to the terminal, he kept repeating, "I killed her." We gave him a couple of days off to recover mentally. When he did return to work some three days later, *we decided* we were not going to put him back on the road. We worked with the union to allow us to switch him with the dock person for the next few days. I emphasize that *we decided* because we did not ask the driver how he was doing or if he wanted to work the dock. That would have been futile. He would have tried to suppress his grief through denial, asserting that he was fine. We reached out to the coroner's office to better understand the cause of death. Fortunately, the coroner was willing to share with us that the young women swerved because a drunk driver struck her. In fact, she didn't swerve; she had careened off the drunk driver before crossing the median and hitting our truck. She had died instantly from the first impact and therefore was dead before she hit our truck. This knowledge was critical to helping our driver get his life back.

You may be thinking, "This wasn't grieving. He didn't experience a loss. This was simply shock." These would be reasonable statements. However, as we will discuss in a future chapter, any time a person experiences trauma or even drama in their life, they go through the grieving process. Let's explore this particular situation a little further.

Was my driver in denial and angry, stages one and two of the model? You bet he was. He kept saying how he couldn't believe this had happened, and he was angry at himself for not reacting to avoid her. Then he would realize that because it all happened so fast and it was dark and raining, there was little he could do, and the cycle would start over again.

Did he bargain? He sure did. I cannot tell you how many times I heard him say, "If only I had done this" or "If only I could have seen her coming."

Was he depressed? His depression took the path of drinking. He later admitted to me that he had spent his days off work and the weekend that followed in a drunken and marijuana-induced stupor.

Finally, acceptance came when the coroner confirmed for him that he was not at fault and had not killed her, but she had died instantly after the first impact. Make no mistake about it; I am sure he continued to relive this horrible, traumatic event over and over and over during the months and years ahead, but those ten days or so that I described above helped him to heal. Whether you realize it or not, how you lead an employee through this tough time in their life will either help them heal or will hinder their progress through the stages of grief. That is the real point of this book.

Let's talk now about some hardcore, tactical do's and don'ts of how your leadership should change during these times.

Should you attend the funeral services? After all, you won't know anybody who will be in attendance except your employee. Having been in the death care business, I am very sensitive to how often people underestimate the value of attending the funeral. Funerals are not for the dead; they are for the living. Trust me, your employee will never forget you were there, and it will help set the stage for how your role as the leader will change. Attending the funeral will help pave the way for you to be more involved and supportive when the associate returns to work. It will help to set the stage for the discussions you will need to have down the road. Let me provide an example.

There was a motorcycle rally in Cincinnati, Ohio. It was a fundraiser for a charitable organization. Hundreds of bikers participated in the annual event. On this particular Saturday, tragedy struck. Somehow, through circumstances that are still unclear to me, some thirty bikes wound up in a pileup. One of our employees was involved. He worked in the factory. I didn't know him well, but I did know him. When his bike went down, his wife was thrown. Although she had a helmet on, she hit her head with enough force to put her in a coma. She died several days later from the brain swelling. My CFO, my director of human resources, and I, as the president, attended the funeral. When we approached our coworker in the receiving line, he broke down and cried. He hugged me like I have never been hugged before. While his words said, "you didn't need to come," his actions said, "thank you so much for being here for me." We heard later from other employees how much he appreciated us being there and how much it meant to him. I ran into him years later while shopping for a new car, of all places. He was with his new fiancée. One of the first things he said to me was how he never forgot our attending his wife's funeral and how much that meant to him personally and what it said about the company. How, in that moment, he knew we cared about him. In conclusion: yes, attend the funeral or memorial services if possible.

Don't treat your employee like nothing has happened. For everyone's sake, don't ignore the elephant in the room. Grief wraps its victim in chains. It attempts to make the person feel isolated, as if they are the only one who has ever experienced such a loss. The more you ignore what is happening, the more isolated the person will feel.

While we are not advocating engaging in daily discussions about what the person is experiencing, you do need to engage in those discussions periodically. Do this even though the discussions will be uncomfortable and there will likely be tears. Allowing your employee to talk about their experience will help them. In a recent *Harvard Business Review* "Insider" article, research has found that employees want their employers to engage them and talk about mental health issues in the workplace.[3] Grief is a mental health issue if there ever was one.

Finally, adjust your leadership style to fit where your grieving employee is at the time. Get more involved. Communicate more. Follow up more. Lead more. Delegate less. Bring the entire team into the fold to ensure the work gets done and the deadlines met before the grieving associate is behind the eight ball. Remember the imagery of the person being driven to their knees by the rocks of grief. Your job as the leader during these times is to lighten the load, not add more rocks to what your employee is already carrying. This will require you to be proactive and persistent. If you simply ask your employee if they need help, that is an empty gesture. If your company is like most, your culture will have conditioned the employee to believe that asking for help is a sign of weakness or a flaw—something that will be brought up and negatively impact their review. Instead, you as the leader need to go to your employee with the plan. Doing this will open the discussion and help your employee realize you want to help them to excel at work even though they are grieving. You will also be communicating that you care and that you are accepting of the "new normal" that will exist at work for a while. In doing so, your team will rally to pick up the slack. They will understand their role in helping support the grieving coworker. They will value and appreciate you and the organization. This is the only effective way forward.

Let me share an emotional and compelling true story of how an organization helped one of its employees excel through her time of grief. For purposes of this story, let's call her Becky. This story is shared with Becky's permission. Becky's husband was diagnosed with cancer some four years earlier. On a routine cancer check, new markers were found in his bloodwork. His cancer had returned, and it was aggressive. He began treatments, but to no avail. Over the next year he would continue to decline. While he was going through his treatments, the company Becky worked for was also going through a transformation, and Becky was told she had to reapply and be interviewed for her job. All employees had to do this, and there was no guarantee of employment. Becky was scared.

Fortunately, Becky's direct supervisor, and I am guessing the organization, had created a culture that made Becky feel safe going to him and sharing her very real fears of being an unemployed, widowed parent. He did all he could to console her and let her know how valuable she was to him and the organization, but he obviously could not make any promises. Throughout the process, he was proactive in accommodating her need to work from home or from her husband's hospital bedside. He engaged Becky in discussions of assignments and proposed alternatives to spreading the work across the team. Becky went through the interviews and shared with her husband that she was not sure how they went. Her husband went into hospice care. In what would be the final week of his life, Becky got a call from her supervisor who said, "Look, I am getting ahead of myself here, but you are likely going to get an offer. I can't guarantee anything, nor do I know for sure when the offer will come. I just wanted you to know."

Within a couple of hours of that call, Becky received another call. This one was from her HR leader. The woman on the other end of the phone said, "I am calling because we wanted you to know that you will be receiving an offer over the next couple of days. While it is a bit uncustomary for us to signal such things to people, we wanted you to know that you will have a job, and you will have a job for as long as you would like to work for us." Then she said something surprising. She asked, "Are you with your husband?" Becky said yes. The voice on the other end of the phone then said, "The reason I called you was because we wanted you to be able to tell your husband the news so he will no longer have to worry about whether or not you have a job."

Her husband passed within a day or two of this conversation. The organization and the team continued to support Becky through her early days of grief. They continued to adapt her workload and schedule to fit her physical and emotional needs. Today she is coming up on two years since her husband died. As she tearfully shared this story with my brother and me, she said, "This organization has my commitment and loyalty for life. They made it possible for me to actually excel at work while I was grieving."

That is caring leadership on every level. That is adaptive leadership on every level. That is the goal of this book. No one waited for Becky to ask. No one waited for Becky to fail or struggle with her performance. No one pretended it was business as usual. No one ignored the reality of the situation.

Unfortunately, this is not the norm, but we hope that through this book and our efforts, this will become somewhat of a movement and the norm will change. If it is to change, however, we are going to have to stop assuming that helping employees through their time of grief is not part of our leadership roles.

A reader wrote to the *New York Times* in January 2020 to describe how they had recently lost a former boss who was also a friend and mentor. They wrote because they felt their current boss was not supportive during a time when they were struggling. The boss fell into the classic trap of avoidance. Rather than engage this person and adapt his leadership to the new reality of this person's situation, the boss was simply conducting business as usual. The person continued to say how they felt isolated and ignored. This piece clearly highlights the need for this book. What really saddened us, however, was contained in the response the paper provided to this person. While there was some good advice given to seek the help of a grief counselor and set up a meeting with the supervisor to discuss the situation, the responding party also conveyed, very clearly, that the person was expecting too much from their leader. The response clearly stated that the leader's job was to make sure the work gets done, not to help employees deal with emotional issues.

We should expect more from our leaders than to just manage a grieving employee as they always have. Unfortunately, the person who wrote in is likely to become part of the $75 billion productivity loss associated with grieving employees and will probably wind up leaving this organization.

Leading Grieving Employees Chapter Summary

- An employee who experiences an emotionally traumatic event will enter the stages of grief described in chapter 3.
- Emotionally traumatized employees are not the same people when they return to work as they were before the incident occurred.

- Employees experiencing the stages of grief will shift down and to the left on the adaptive leadership matrix.

- Most company cultures make employees feel they cannot ask for help or admit they are struggling emotionally.

- Adapting your leadership style and proactively engaging with the employee in the grief process is how leaders help grieving employees excel at work and minimize the cost of lost productivity.

- The rest of the team will want to help and will look to the leader for guidance on the best way to support the grieving employee.

"A leader, first and foremost, is human. Only when we have the strength to show our vulnerability can we truly lead."

—Simon Senik

CHAPTER 9

The Person in the Mirror *

Learn what to do when the leader is the person returning
to work after an emotionally traumatizing event
(Anthony Casablanca)

To this point in the book we have discussed the stages of grief. We have talked about how the depth of a relationship, coupled with the modality of the loss, impacts the depth of grief one experiences. We have also given you a framework to guide when and how you, as the leader, will need to adapt your leadership style to meet the challenges of leading a person who is trapped in the despair and depression of the early stages of grief. But what happens when it is you, the leader, who experiences the loss? What if you are the one trapped in the heavily weighted chains of grief?

On the one hand, you could hope that your leader has read this book and adapts their style of leading to meet you in your new normal. That would be great, but what if they haven't read the book? Or what if you are the CEO, sitting on top of the leadership pyramid, with no one above you to guide and support you? Are you supposed to hide your grief and just suck it up? Are you supposed to ignore your pain, throw yourself into your work, and carry on like nothing has changed? Repressed grief can be disastrous. Your work can only fill so many hours of the day. At some point, you have to be alone. And alone, you will face the reality of your loss and feel the pain. So what can you do?

We would suggest that you apply the concepts we discussed in the last two chapters to help you to admit and show your vulnerability and to help grow your people. The reality is that your people don't grow magically into their roles. While some of their growth occurs simply through time in the role, the more significant growth comes from being stretched—from being asked to take on tasks or responsibilities beyond the normal bounds of their role. If you think about the concepts of stewardship, trust, and empowerment, those traits all grow as the employee is given the ability to demonstrate they can step up to the tasks and have the agility to learn new skills. Often, as leaders, we hinder our people from reaching their full potential because of the restrictions we place on them. I can't tell you how many times I have had to remind people I coach that they were in their current role because their leader allowed them to grow with a stretch assignment—one that they perhaps did not feel they were ready to handle. Now here they are, a senior leader at an incredibly young age, with the opportunity to extend the same growth opportunity to one of their people, and what do they do? They say, "I don't think they're ready."

Many times, it is the leader who is not ready for growth, not the employee. The leader is not prepared to adapt their style to meet what would become the new needs of the employee given the stretch assignment. One of my favorite quotes is from Stephen Covey. In his book *The 7 Habits of Highly Successful People*, he says, "In order to be trustworthy, first you have to be trusted." Think about this powerful concept for a moment. A big part of leadership is about growing your people. You can either wait for them to demonstrate stewardship and trustworthiness, or you can trust them with new assignments and let them grow into a new level of stewardship, trust, empowerment, and collaboration. To do the latter, you will have to adapt your leadership style to fit their new needs. You will have to adapt your leadership style to meet them where they will be under the demands of the new assignment. In this regard, leadership is like a rhythmic dance. When done well, it is a smooth, almost invisible transition of the leader moving in and out, communicating more and less frequently, empowering more and less, trusting more and less, helping that employee to grow in the process.

I can think of at least three career-defining assignments I was handed that I would never have considered requesting. In fact, when the conversations to take on the assignments occurred, it made me sick to my stomach and sent fear throughout my mind and body. The first was when I was asked to relocate to our largest manufacturing facility and assume the role of plant controller in a struggling plant. I was twenty-five years old at the time and didn't have a clue what the role really entailed. The work was hard, the hours were long, and the stress levels were high. I later wound up running that facility. The second was when the president of the company asked me to lead a cross-functional discount team to figure out how to manage this ever-growing expenditure. I was an accountant and an operations person. I knew nothing about the commercial side of our business. Nothing about pricing or discount structures. The work that team did changed the future course of the business. What was most amazing was that the president of the company at the time gave me free access to his calendar. He would meet with me at any time. All I had to do was ask. I was a director at the time, three levels below him. Nonetheless, he adapted his leadership style to collaborate and communicate more frequently with me, as did several "mentors" I recruited for that assignment.

The third was when I was the vice president of human resources. We were in a succession planning meeting, discussing who should be listed to succeed the vice president of manufacturing. After much discussion, the president of the company turned to me and said, "I think we should put your name down as the successor." I thought I was going to pass out. I hadn't been in manufacturing for over a decade at that point. The company had made great strides in continuous improvement and lean thinking, and I had not attended any of the formal training sessions or trips to Japan afforded the functional leaders. Six months later, I was made the head of manufacturing. A year later we rolled the distribution function up under my role, and my first lean cultural transformation was underway. Two years after that, I was made an operating company president.

I do not cite these examples to brag; I bring them up to point out that I was technically not ready to assume any of these roles. It would have been so easy for all those involved in the decisions to have said, "Boy, I don't know. I don't think he is ready." That is not, however, what they did. Instead, they placed trust in me and allowed my stewardship, trust, empowerment, and collaboration traits to grow. They allowed me to become trustworthy.

The point here is to lay the foundation for how you can use the models of the previous chapters to help you lead if you are the griever. Earlier I said that leadership is about growing your people. Leadership is also about being vulnerable. While many may think being vulnerable is a sign of weakness, I can assure you that vulnerability and weakness are not interchangeable words. Being vulnerable means letting those around you know that you don't have all the answers. That you are human. And in the case of trauma, that you are hurting and will need their help to make sure you do not become a barrier to the team's progress. Having the strength and courage to be vulnerable has another benefit as well. A leader who demonstrates vulnerability is establishing a culture of safety for their people. They are, by their example, telling their people that it is okay not to know it all. It's okay to need help. It's okay to have the courage to ask for help and to be vulnerable. You will be amazed how much more resilient, more engaged, more committed, and more productive your team will become when the leader establishes this type of culture.

As a leader, you are always setting an example, every minute of every day. Sometimes you do this intentionally, but often it happens even when you think no one is watching. By embracing your grief or the grief others are experiencing and sharing it with your people, you will be setting a powerful example for others to do the same if they ever encounter a similar situation. By setting this example, you will be promoting a culture of compassion, kinship, and teamwork that will bring your team closer. It will help to send a clear message that it's okay to grieve here. That being a part of this team means you are a part of a safe and supportive environment at work.

While this chapter makes it seem like you will be experiencing things in a vacuum, that is far from the truth. The truth is that your people will want to help, but they will not know what to do or how to approach you. They will fall victim to all the mistakes we talked about in previous chapters. They are going to try to provide understanding and comfort, but they will say all the wrong things. You will tolerate these things, but some of them will sadden you and make you angry. They will say things like, "Your loved one is in a better place," or "At least you had X number of years together," or that ever-popular "At least they died doing something they loved." You will fall prey to all the emotions, confusion, fog, anger, and tearful moments that we have talked about earlier. There is a phrase often used these days: "lean in." It might have been popularized by a previous book by Sheryl Sandberg. We would give you that same advice. "Lean in" to your grief as a leader.

What does that mean? It means acknowledge the grief, don't bury it. It means share your grief, don't hide it. It means bring your team into your grief, don't shut them out. Just like you needed to make a proactive plan for how the work was going to get done when an employee of yours was grieving, you now need to allow your people to do the same for you. You accomplish this by leaning into the situation and leaning on your people. They will do amazing things if you will let them support you. They will grow and be better for it in the long run, and so will you.

Let's revisit our talent matrix from the previous chapters, but this time, let's assume it is you and not Nikki, who is experiencing the trauma. Let's say you are at work when your wife calls to tell you that she has found a lump in her breast and is going to the doctor. Suddenly, your normal day at the office comes to a crashing halt. The moment takes your breath away, and you know this could only be the beginning of a long emotional roller coaster. You begin to feel what grief experts would call "anticipatory grief" as your mind races through all the possibilities. Within a week, your fears become a reality. You and your family are in a battle to defeat this hidden disease that now has a name and a treatment protocol. You begin to go through the stages of grief. You know you will need to spend large amounts of time out of the office. In your heart you wish that you didn't have to work at all. You may even question why any of it matters. These would all be very natural thoughts and emotions.

Fortunately, you have an excellent team of people around you, and you have tried to build a culture that is open, honest, caring, and allows for vulnerability. The first thing you do is call your team into your office to explain the situation to them. You get choked up as you try to hold back the tears that are building in your eyes. There is a collective gasp as your team comprehends what you are telling them. The first thing out of their mouths is "What can we do to help?"

You tell Nikki, your high-potential person, and the one most likely to be your successor at some point, that you will need her to take on some of your role and attend some of the meetings you would typically attend. You tell Bob, who is still coming up the learning curve, to go to John, your high performer, for guidance when you are not in the office or available. You tell John to take over the day-to-day running of the team. This should free you up to be with your wife and help her through her chemotherapy treatments and the debilitating effects she will experience in between appointments. Before leaving the room, several of your team ask if they can hug you.

We probably all know leaders who have handled situations like this similarly. We might also know people who have either left their spouses to fend for themselves because they felt they were irreplaceable at work. Or leaders who allowed their team and department to struggle to figure things out in their absence, leading to performance and productivity issues.

You might be asking yourself, "Why wouldn't I have gone to my boss first?" You might have done so, depending on the type of leader they are. If you work for a command-and-control, never-show-weakness kind of leader, you might feel you have to go to them first. However, if that is the case, you likely would not feel you could then empower your team. You might feel that you will have to suck it up and figure out how to be present both at work and for your wife. That is a situation easier said than done, and frankly, it never works well. If that is the culture you work in, we would recommend going to your leader with the news along with the plan for how your team will cover for you.

I would encourage you to search YouTube for Col. Arthur Athens's keynote address delivered at the 2010 USNA (United States Naval Academy) Leadership Conference, Part 2. The address is about an hour-long, but there is a twelve-minute segment that specifically covers the topic of a grieving leader. In the video, Col. Athens describes a time during his command when his newborn son died as the result of a required heart surgery. He describes how he leaned into his grief and leaned on his people, allowing himself to become vulnerable at that moment. He also describes how his team responded and how they grew. Col. Athens is a remarkable person. I will speak about him more in a later chapter. If he could be vulnerable in a military setting, I am sure you can as well in your organization.

The Person in the Mirror Chapter Summary

- Often it is the leader who hinders the growth of their people because of the restrictions we place on them.
- The demonstrated attributes of stewardship, trust, empowerment, collaboration, and communication frequency all improve as the employee learns new skills and takes on new challenges.
- The adaptive leadership model discussed in chapters 7 and 8 can be used to help the leader who is struggling through the grief process.
- Great leaders are not afraid to show their vulnerability, and through that vulnerability, they create a culture of safety for their people.
- Your people will want to help you through your struggle but won't know what to do.
- Great leaders let their people engage in their grief and allow them to take on more responsibility, which leads to growth.
- Learn about the power of being a vulnerable leader by searching YouTube for Col. Arthur Athens's keynote address at the 2010 United States Naval Academy leadership conference entitled "What's Love Got To Do With It."

"When our days become dreary with low hovering clouds of despair, and when our nights become darker than a thousand midnights, let us remember that there is a creative force in this universe, working to pull down the gigantic mountains of evil, a power that is able to make a way out of no way and transform dark yesterdays into bright tomorrows."

—Martin Luther King Jr.

CHAPTER 10
Other Types of Loss

Learn how your company's initiatives can create
emotionally traumatizing events for employees
(Anthony Casablanca)

Throughout the book we have given many examples of losses. Some are from personal experience, and others are ones we have witnessed. Most of those examples have dealt with an actual death that has occurred. However, if you do any type of search on change management, you will quickly run across some adapted version of the Kübler-Ross five-stage model of grief. It may have some steps added, or it may have some of the names of the stages changed, but the images will, at their core, be based on the grief model. Why is that? The reason is that anytime we experience a loss, we grieve. That loss could be as significant as the loss of a loved one, or it could be as trivial as failing a test or getting a speeding ticket. You might wonder if these examples take the grief model too far. Do they?

The next time your teenage child fails a high-school exam or receives a bad grade in one of their classes, watch how they react. I'll bet it is something like this.

Denial: "I can't believe I am failing! I pay attention, go to class, take notes, and study. I don't know what else to do."

Anger: "I can't believe this is happening. It's the teacher. He sucks and doesn't teach the stuff that is on the exams. He wants us to fail. The average grade in the class was a 72. I hate this stupid class anyway, and it doesn't have anything to do with what I want to do in life. When am I ever going to need to balance a chemical equation?"

Bargaining: "Please, God, help me pass this class. Help me figure this out. I know, I'll talk to the teacher and tell him I will do anything to get my grades up. Maybe I can do some extra assignments or something for extra credit.

Depression: "If I don't get this grade up, I won't graduate, and I won't get into Harvard!" (Bargaining and depression will likely come at the same time in this example.)

Acceptance: "I have to pass this class. If I can just get a 75 on the next two exams, I will be able to raise my grade to a passing level. Surely I can get a 75 if I study more and find someone to help me with this stupid stuff. Plus, the teacher said there would be a curve. I can do this."

Does this sound familiar? Even though this transpires over hours or days, your child progressed through the five stages of grief.

Considering this, what do you think your employees feel in any of the following situations?

You announce a reduction in force, or a "right-sizing." Not only are the impacted individuals going to go through these five stages of grief, but so will a portion of the larger organization. Why? Because the remaining employees will wonder if they are next. That is no different a mental place than my brother and I coming to the realization that, as the oldest generation now, we are the "next to go" in our family.

You acquire a company. You can bet that while your employees may be excited, the employees at the acquired company are scared. They are in denial that the company is no longer going to be family-owned. They will be angry at their leadership team for "selling out." They will be scared of what changes are coming, and they won't trust you. The same will be true when two public companies merge.

You close a plant. I have firsthand experience with this, and I was fortunate enough to be working for a remarkable human resources leader who innately seemed to know that we needed to lead differently after the announcement. We had a plant in the Northeast that, through no fault of any of our people, needed to be closed. It was an old four-story, landlocked building with no ability to expand. It sat in a neighborhood that had imposed regulations prohibiting the running of the plant on the second shift, and the environmental restrictions were no longer manageable. As a result, 192 people found themselves faced with the stark realization that they would be out of work, and there was nothing they could do about it. How did we lead differently during this time?

First, against the wishes of many, we gave the employees twelve months' notice. We decided to trust in our people and the fact that if they felt we were being fair and compassionate with them, they would act responsibly and not revert to violence, vandalism, or sabotage. We were right.

Second, we were present. My boss asked me to fly up to the facility to be on-site every other week until the plant closed. Initially I was there to explain benefits and observe. However, after the first month, I was present to listen, guide, and assist people as they navigated the life-changing decisions that lay ahead of them.

Finally, we worked with the local Department of Labor to secure as many advantages, benefits, and opportunities for our people as possible. Realizing that workers with an average age in their mid-fifties were probably not familiar with resume building, networking, or job hunting, I assumed a primary role of trying to bring the opportunities to our people. We held on-site job fairs and brought other employers in the area to our site to interview our workers.

We also plotted all our people on a matrix like the one we laid out in earlier chapters. Why? Because my boss wanted us to try to identify those individuals at the highest risk of failure. Stated another way, he wanted us to try to identify those people who would likely get stuck in the grief cycle, too gripped by denial, anger, and depression to help themselves through the process. My job was to seek those people out and pay special attention to them—to engage them, listen to them, and help them.

To make a long story short, all 192 people either had found jobs or retired by the time the plant closed. The local union couldn't believe how we treated our people and them in the process. There were times when I worked with government officials on behalf of the union. The representative from the Department of Labor publicly stated that if every company treated their people this way when closing a plant, his job would be much easier, and the lives of those impacted would be significantly improved.

What was it that we really did? Without formally realizing it, we worked the model in this book. We coached and supported our people more than they would have ever asked of us. We proactively intervened to ensure our people were taken care of and that productivity would not suffer. You see, throughout this entire twelve-month period, the plant continued to achieve all of its safety, quality, cost, and production goals. It accomplished this while our people were grieving the loss of their livelihood and worrying about the futures of their families and how they would earn a living moving forward. And that is the real point of this book. To help you, as a leader, strike an appropriate balance between the natural process of grief and the need to maintain productivity.

When you consider that ERP system you are upgrading or changing, or indeed anything in the workplace that introduces change, while most of the changes will not require the kind of intervention and adaptation of your leadership style that we have talked about in this book, they will cause people to go through the five stages of grief nonetheless.

By the way, the loss of a pet is right up there on the list. Our pets have transitioned from mere animals that help around the farm to full-blown family members. I know that both my brother and I grieved more than we ever thought we would when we had to put down our dogs. Personally, it was much harder than I ever thought it would be, and I was more distracted and cried more than I ever thought I would have.

Other Types of Loss Chapter Summary

- Any search of the topic of change management will lead you to examples of stages of grief model.

- Any time an individual or team encounters a change to their current reality, they can experience an emotionally traumatic event and slip into a state of grief.

- Your company initiatives can trigger such changes and cause individuals, teams, or even your entire organization to grieve.

- The adaptive leadership process will help you lead through these situations with care and compassion and will minimize the productivity loss associated with grieving employees.

"You can never over-communicate enough as a leader at a company, but at a remote company, nothing could be truer. Because you don't physically see people in-person, information doesn't spread in the same way, so leaders need to do the heavy lifting for evangelizing the message."

— Claire Lew, Know Your Team

CHAPTER 11
Leading Remotely

Learn how working remotely requires leaders who are even more adept at using the Adaptive Leadership model
(Anthony Casablanca)

W e have covered many concepts throughout this book. We have discussed how the level of trauma, or grief, a person experiences is directly related to how close the person is to the event circumstances and how sudden or tragic the event. We have also discussed the five stages of grief and how they affect a person's emotional well-being and performance at work. We then covered, in great detail, the adaptive leadership model, demonstrating how great leaders are those who adapt their leadership style to meet the development needs of their people. Through this discussion, we also explained the impact grief has on the performance and potential of an employee when they return to work after an emotionally traumatizing event occurs and how you, as the leader, need to engage in the process to minimize the impact on productivity. However, we have also given the impression that these behaviors only play out or are only useful in an office setting, leaving you wondering how to apply these concepts in a work from home or remote leadership environment.

Rest assured, these concepts all still apply. In fact, your adaptive leadership skills will be even more critical when leading remotely. Adaptive leadership is about being present and engaging in the moment. The irony is that being present and engaging does not require a physical presence. It does, however, require the leader to intentionally engage in the emotional well-being of their employees in authentic, sincere, and heartfelt ways.

I was recently watching a Simon Sinek video, where he described the impact a handwritten note has on people. In the video, he talks about how the exact same words typed in an email versus put in a handwritten note totally change the feelings of the reader simply because the one is handwritten. The same principle holds when leading people remotely. Ironically, your physical presence is the least essential component of being present. The power of being present comes from the connection that occurs when your employee realizes you cared enough to engage them on a personal, heartfelt, compassionate level that is not self-serving. The power of being present in the moment comes when your employee, or employees, realize you are taking the extra step. That you are putting yourself in a vulnerable place by demonstrating you care about them. It's the handwritten note versus sending an email effect.

Having been on both sides of remote leadership, I know how easy it is to fall into the trap of sending emails and voicemails. You don't have to change your schedule to work around the time differences, and if it is a complicated subject, you don't have to deal with any push back or emotion, or at least it can be postponed. I can also tell you that is not leadership. Leading remotely requires you to lead more, not less. If I could give you one phrase to help guide you in times of having to lead remote teams, it would be *next level leadership*. Whatever steps you are thinking about to engage your employee or team, take it to the next level. An example may help to illustrate the point.

An employee's wife is diagnosed with late-stage lymphoma and requires both surgery and chemotherapy. They have two young children who need care and attention. The couple arranges for her mother to stay with them to help out, but your employee needs flexibility to get his wife to the treatments and to be present for the children. The employee is responsible for the finances of your global operations and would be in the upper right-hand box of the adaptive leadership matrix. He is clearly a high performing, high potential. The employee and the leader would typically have many personal interactions during the day to tackle both tactical execution and strategic issues. Recognizing the employee is emotionally traumatized and entering the stages of grief as a result of this event, the leader engages him in his time of need and helps him to shift priorities and responsibilities and enable him to work from home when needed. To facilitate the transition, the leader increases the communication frequency with this individual, so the two of them can stay on the same page. On this day, the leader has scheduled a video conference for their update. Once the call begins, the employee immediately jumps into the business at hand and starts providing his update. The leader, whether formally trained or intuitively, stops the conversation in its tracks and begins to ask how the employee's wife is doing? How are the kids dealing with the family crisis? How is the employee holding up? As the update draws to a close, the discussion turns to an upcoming strategic planning meeting that will require the employee to travel internationally. As the two of them discuss the meeting, the leader makes it clear that the meeting can be postponed until the timing is better for the employee. The employee explains that the timing of the conference falls between chemo sessions, so he should be able to attend and conduct the meeting.

As I listened to this story, the following points stood out to me as clear demonstrations of the principles we have discussed in this book.

- It became clear that all the topics of the meeting could have been handled through an email update. However, the leader decided for personal engagement instead.
- The leader chose a medium for the update that not only allowed him to hear the tone of the employee's voice, but also allowed him to see the employee's body language.
- The leader engaged the employee in the emotionally charged and uncomfortable conversation about his wife's condition and how the family was dealing with the situation.
- The leader made it clear that further work modifications could be made to assist the family further if the employee felt they were needed.

While this leader demonstrated these behaviors instinctively, this is how all leaders should respond. By the way, the leader, also called the employee the day of his travel to the conference and reinforced that it was not too late to cancel the meeting. Telling him, "I don't care if you are checked in and through security, if you feel you need to be home, or if your wife calls you, I expect you to turn around and go home." That is an example of being present. That is an example leading more, not less.

Leading Remotely Chapter Summary

- Leading remote teams requires more leadership, not less.
- Being present does not require a physical presence.
- However the remote leader is thinking about engaging the emotionally traumatized employee, they should take that engagement to the next level.
- Voice communication will be better than email, and video communication will be better than just voice because it allows the leader to hear the voice inflections and see the non-verbal cues the employee is communicating.

"An idea not coupled with action will never get any bigger than the brain cell it occupied."

—*Arnold Glasow,* businessman and
author of *Glasow's Gloombusters*

CHAPTER 12
Now What?

The call to action. Leading with courage and compassion
(Anthony Casablanca)

We hope that this book has provided you with some insight into a function of leadership that, much like loss itself, few people ever discuss. We hope the information in this book will help make you an even more effective leader than you already are. We hope that if you find yourself in a situation where your people are engulfed in the five stages of grief, you will be able to recognize it and adapt your leadership style appropriately. By doing so, you will be able to help them return to work and reduce the impact their grieving will have on the productivity of your team, function, department, or organization.

There are three words we would like for you to remember: Competence. Courage. Compassion. I had the honor to hear retired Col. Arthur Athens speak on two separate occasions. Col. Athens speaks about the three "C"s of leadership[1] and the questions the entire organization is looking for every leader to answer. By everyone, he means those above you as well as those below you.

The first "C" is *competence*. People do not necessarily expect a leader to be a technical expert, but they do expect a leader to have a basic understanding of the skills required of the team they are leading. If they do not possess such an understanding, then the team will look to see if the leader is working hard to gain that understanding. If the leader is doing so, the team will be surprisingly forgiving around this issue.

The second "C" is *courage*. Here the team or organization is looking closely at how the leader behaves to determine if the leader will always do the right thing. Will they make the right decisions even when those decisions are hard, will cause disruption, or even negatively impact the leader?

The third "C" is *compassion*. The compassion question is simple. Does this leader care about me, or are they only out for themselves? While every leader has to continually balance what is good for the employees with what is good for the stakeholders and what is good for the company, striking that balance can always be done in a caring and compassionate way if the leader truly cares about their people.

While the question of competence may not directly apply to the discussions in this book, we think the questions of courage and compassion do. This is how. When one of your people experiences a loss that rocks their world to its core—when they are fully in the grip of grieving and are struggling through its five stages—the question is this: Will you as a leader have the courage and compassion to get involved? Will you have the courage and compassion to adapt your leadership style to help them through the process? Will you have the courage and compassion to break out the box of Kleenex and be willing to allow that person to show their emotion when they need to? Will you have the courage and compassion to recognize that they will not ask for help, but that you should coach and support them without their asking? Or will you just assume that because they are now back at work, they should just suck it up and return to business as usual? While on the surface the choice seems simple and clear, the reality is that one is much harder than the other. One is more rewarding than the other. One is more "productive" than the other.

Now What Chapter Summary

- Competence, courage, and compassion are three words we would like you to remember from this chapter.
- Leading grieving or emotionally traumatized employees requires that you adapt your leadership style to meet the employee in their newfound reality.

- Leading grieving or emotionally traumatized employees requires that you lead with a new level of courage and compassion.
- Great leaders have the courage and compassion to engage the employee and proactively coach and support them without their asking.
- Grieving employees can excel at work when the leader adapts their style to the employee's new reality.

MORE ABOUT THE AUTHORS

Driven by their passion for helping others grow and develop, Anthony and Guy decided to combine their experience and expertise in the creation of this work. As they researched this topic and heard the stories of those they interviewed, their passion became a mission. As a result, Anthony and Guy cofounded GriefLeaders LLC. GriefLeaders is a training and consulting organization with the sole purpose of educating leaders and providing them with a process to follow, enabling them to help grieving employees excel at work.

The GriefLeaders training process consists of three steps, which, when implemented, will reduce the impact of lost productivity from grieving or emotionally traumatized employees.

Step one is the completion of an emotional well-being cultural assessment. In this step, we review policies and procedures and interview both past grieving employees and leaders to determine how well-aligned leaders are with how the organization expects its leaders to behave when leading emotionally traumatized employees.

Step two is to construct a personalized leadership training session. In this session, leaders will develop the skills necessary to use the Adaptive Leadership model within the construct of your organization. This step also includes an Adaptive Leadership assessment to help leaders see areas in which they may need to focus in order to successfully lead emotionally traumatized employees.

Step three of the process consists of personal coaching for leaders who participate in the sessions. In this step, Anthony and Guy will provide coaching to those leaders who find themselves thrust into having to lead in these often awkward, uncomfortable, and emotional situations.

Visit us at www.griefleaders.com to begin the process with a complimentary consultation.

ACKNOWLEDGMENTS

While there are too many people who have impacted our lives and the creation of this book to mention, there are a few who we would like to acknowledge.

Mary and Clayton Mathile have provided continued support and guidance to both Guy and I over the past forty years. They were the first people we turned to for advice on how to move our seed of an idea to a book and ultimately to GriefLeaders.

My relationship with P. Douglas (Doug) Wilson started when I interviewed him as a potential new boss. Our relationship quickly transitioned from a boss to a mentor, and a friend. We cannot thank Doug enough for connecting us to some incredible people who served as invaluable advisors to Guy and me throughout this process.

To Ken Jennings, John Stall-Wart, and Mark DeLuzio. You were invaluable coaches throughout the process, not only offering your experience and advice but also allowing us to stand on your shoulders rather than having to start at the very bottom as novice authors.

To all the leaders we have encountered throughout our careers who served to teach both leadership and life lessons. We will not name you individually for fear of leaving someone off the list. However, we would like to thank you for being examples to us, frequently without your even being aware we were watching or paying attention.

We would also like to acknowledge the many people we encountered throughout the writing of this book who shared their time and emotional stories with us. You helped to make this book real for us.

NOTES AND REFERENCES

Introduction

1) In 2017, a total of 2,813,503 resident deaths were registered in the United States-https://www.cdc.gov/nchs/products/databriefs/db328.htm

2) Every 13 seconds, there is one divorce in America. That equates to 277 divorces per hour, 6,646 divorces per day, 46,523 divorces per week, and 2,419,196 divorces per year. https://www.wf-lawyers.com/divorce-statistics-and-facts/

3) In 2018, an estimated 1,735,350 new cases of cancer will be diagnosed in the United States. https://www.cancer.gov/about-cancer/understanding/statistics

4) Experts say the United States is in the throes of an opioid epidemic. An estimated 10.3 million Americans aged 12 and older misused opioids in 2018, including 9.9 million prescription pain reliever abusers and 808,000 heroin users. https://www.cnn.com/2017/09/18/health/opioid-crisis-fast-facts/index.html

5) The Grief Recovery Institute Educational Foundation. (2003). Grief Index: the Hidden Annual Costs of Grief in America's Workplace http://grief.net/Articles/The_Grief_Index_2003.pdf

Chapter 1: Moribund

Chapter 2: Types of Losses

Chapter 3: The Stages of Grief

1) Elisabeth Kübler-Ross (July 8, 1926 – August 24, 2004) was a Swiss-American psychiatrist, a pioneer in near-death studies, and author of the internationally best-selling book, On Death and Dying (1969), where she first discussed

her theory of the five stages of grief, also known as the "Kübler-Ross model." Published by MacMillan and Company

Chapter 4: The Funeral Process
General Social Survey conducted in 2014 and cited in a Religious News article ReligiousNews.com/2015/03/12. Study conducted by Tobin Grant (<u>http://</u> <u>tobingrant.religiousnews.com/2014/08/05the-great-decline-61-years-of-</u> <u>religion-religiosity-in-one-graph-2013-hits-a-new-low/</u>)

Adapted from a National Funeral Director's Association study (https://iogar. memberclicks.net/assets/docs/2015%20nfda%20cremation%20and%20 burial%20report.pdf)

Chapter 5: The Need For Preventative Measures

Chapter 6: The Role of Aftercare

Chapter 7: Adaptive Leadership

Chapter 8: The Art of Leading Employees Through Grief
"Option B Facing Adversity, Building Resilience and Finding Joy" by Sheryl Sandberg and Adam Grant. Alfred A Knopf; New York; 2017

Celeste Roberge "Rising Cairn" also sometimes referred to "The Weight of Grief"- http://www.celesteroberge.com/w-cairn-rising.php

Harvard Business Review reprint H056G0 published on HBR.org October 7, 2017. "Research: People Want Their Employers To Talk About Mental Health" by Kelly Greenwood, Vivek Bapat, and Mike Mughan

Chapter 9: The Person in the Mirror

Chapter 10: Other Types of Loss

Chapter 11: Adaptive Leadership in a Work From Home World

Chapter 12: Now What

1) Colonel Athens is the Naval Academy's first Distinguished Military Professor of Leadership. He has a diverse background, spanning the military, higher education, and the non-profit sector. To view his talk in its entirety on YouTube search Col. Arthur Athens's keynote address delivered at the 2010 USNA (United States Naval Academy) Leadership Conference,